WENDELL L. WILLKIE

WENDELL WILLKIE
of ELWOOD

by
HERMAN O. MAKEY

NATIONAL BOOK COMPANY, Inc.
Elwood, Indiana

TO EVERY
AMERICAN CITIZEN
WHO ADMIRES

A man of convictions
　　　　who is willing to fight for his convictions;
A man who knows the problems of all groups
　　　　and has sympathy for all groups;
A man who faces today's problems
　　　　with today's techniques . . . . . .

　　　　　　I dedicate this story of
　　　　　　WENDELL WILLKIE

"The central issue is our power, the people's power, political and economic. . . . Excessive power in the hands of big corporations is an evil. But it is no more evil than excessive power in the hands of big government. As we are opposed to industrial monopoly, so are we opposed to government monopoly."

WENDELL WILLKIE

ILLUSTRATIONS

Lewellyn

The Prophetic Entrance to Willkie's High School

WENDELL WILLKIE

★

In the fertile farmlands of the Mississippi Valley, the alfalfa sends its roots into the amazing depth of fertile soil laid down in the ages of long ago when the ocean covered the plains just now covered by waves of ripening grain. Just so, the character of a man grows out of conditions which he did not make, conditions created by nature during long geological ages; conditions created by events far away, even across ocean and mountain barriers; conditions created by political and social conditions both far and near. Not that mankind is dominated by these conditions, any more than the alfalfa is dominated by the soil and the geological past. The alfalfa makes use of these conditions and is able to draw the nourishment it needs for its specific uses, at the same time enriching the soil through its partnership with the unseen bacteria which it nourishes: man may succumb and may yield himself to the conditions in which he finds himself; or he may use these conditions to develop his abilities and to grow physically, mentally, socially, and spiritually, at the same time returning to his community and to his times an enriching influence due to his

1

contact with the life about him, contacts whose effect may be unseen but by no means unreal.

So, to understand the man Willkie, one must understand the community in which he was born, from which he drew those early influences which are so inescapable throughout the rest of one's life. For no man can see the world through uncolored glasses. The farmer, the merchant, the banker, the housewife, the clerk, the manufacturer, the machinist — every man's outlook upon life is inevitably colored by his experiences, his interests, his successes, his failures, his friends, his hopes and their more or less complete realizations. Fortunate, then, the man whose experiences have been so diversified that his view of life is not colored by one facet of experience so that he sees a world discolored and distorted but whose view is such a combination that it approaches as nearly as possible a true, uncolored one.

Mound Dwellers

Wendell Willkie, "Win" to his many friends, was born into a community, typical of thousands of others in the United States and yet with a personality of its own, where it was natural to see life broadly. Elwood, Indiana, lies in the rich plain of the Mississippi Valley system where the lifegiving soil runs as deep as ninety feet. It has been an inhabited region for untold centuries, for numerous mounds testify that the moundbuilders found it hospitable to life. It was one great forest abounding in the varied fruitage common to this latitude —persimmons, haws, pawpaws, hickory nuts, walnuts, acorns—and also in edible animals—pigeons, turkeys, deer, and bear. Its streams were full of fish, and its marshes contained in abundance numerous species of fur-bearing animals. Certainly, for primitive man, this was a hospitable and inviting area.

INDIANS

When the white man first pushed his way into this district, he found it the home of the Indians. The Miamis laid claim to this region, but such claim was substantiated chiefly by the fact that they were in the majority. The Weas, the Pottawatomies, the Pianka-shaws, the Shawnees all roamed the forest and called it home. When the Delawares, whom the various tribes considered the wisest of the Indian nations, were driven out of what is now the Eastern states by the warlike Five Nations, the Miamis gave them permission to settle in what is now Madison and Delaware counties of Indiana.

The Delawares were the most peaceful of the Indian tribes; and this fact, together with the intermarriage of white traders and settlers into influential Indian families, spared the earlier settlers from the terror and suffering of the first settlers in other parts of what was then known as the West. However, the suspicion and hatred engendered between the Indians and the whites as a result of the unfriendly acts of individuals and small groups throughout the whole region west of the Appalach-ian Mountains ended this period of security; and increas-ing conflicts broke out between the whites and the Indians, whom they were continually pressing westward. These conflicts were encouraged by the French, English,

3

and Spaniards, all of whom hoped to prevent the Americans from taking the lands which they themselves were then too feeble either to defend or conquer.

When the young nations which resulted from the American Revolution united under the Articles of Confederation, one of the pressing causes of antagonism between them was the disposition of the western lands. Finally, these lands were ceded to the National government; and the Ordinance of 1787 established the status of the new lands as partners with and neither the subordinates nor the rivals of the new nation. Just how radical a solution this was is admirably set forth by Theodore Roosevelt in his *Winning of the West*. No other nation had ever permitted this, either making their new colonies subservient to the parent nation or giving them complete independence and so making them potential and, in cases, actual and active rivals.

The most pressing problem relating to the administration of the Northwest Territory so established was that of the Indian relations. The government was weak, since the states had not yet lost their sense of separate independence and the new government had not yet won the confidence of the citizens. Washington knew what measures were necessary to make the region peaceful, but the country was not in the mood to take these measures. So a wavering policy was adopted, as stern as was possible but without definite action. It was still thought by most Americans that a national army was a danger and that peace was worth any price. Generals competent to meet the conditions of Indian warfare were few, the army was small and poorly trained, and

4

the state militia were unreliable and unwilling to undergo military discipline.

So the Indian raids became more and more common and terrible, until Washington decided that definite action had to be taken, regardless of public opinion. General Harmar and General St. Clair were both waylaid because they neglected to take the elementary precautions specifically given them by Washington, and their armies were ignominiously defeated. "Mad" Anthony Wayne was finally assigned the task of subduing the Indians. After careful preparation, including intensive training of his undisciplined army, he marched on the Indians and broke their power at the Battle of Fallen Timbers in 1794. The last resistance of the Indians was broken at the Battle of Tippecanoe by William Henry Harrison in 1811.

TREATIES

During the long conflict with the Indians, numerous treaties were made. The ones which most directly concerned the area in which Elwood is located were the Treaty of Vincennes, in 1804, in which the Piankeshaws gave up all their rights in this area; the Treaty of Grouseland, in 1805, in which "the Pottawatomies, Miamis, Eel Rivers, and Weas explicitly acknowledge the right of the Delawares to sell the tract of land conveyed to the United States by the Treaty of the 18th of August, 1804, which tract was given by the Piankeshaws to the Delawares about thirty-seven years ago"; and the New Purchase Treaty at St. Mary's, Ohio, in 1818, which was the final cession in which the Delawares gave all their lands in Indiana in exchange for lands west of the Mississippi River.

Life of Settlers

Naturally, the first interest of the settlers was to establish homes. The first problem, of course, was to clear the land, no small task even with modern machinery, a task which few today would care to undertake with the limited equipment of the early eighteen hundreds. Wedges, axes, and adzes, with handles renewed by the woodsman himself, were almost his sole equipment except courage, industry, and a faith in and a vision of the future.

Consequently, their homes were simple, for most of the energy of the family was diverted to cutting trees, clearing brush, tilling the soil between the stumps until they could be burned out, splitting rails, making fences, and draining the lowlands. It is impossible for us today to conceive the tremendous physical toil necessary to wrest a livelihood from the soil which now, with the aid of modern tools and by modern methods, produces an abundance so easily. In addition, the settler had to make and repair most of his tools, since transportation from the coast was expensive and took weeks. His wife bore no less a burden of spinning, knitting, sewing, drying grain, curing meat, making candles, and doing the multitude of other tasks which are now performed for her by factories and service shops. Birth control was a thought yet far in the future; and, married often at the age of fifteen or sixteen (She was an "old maid", a term of reproach indicating that she was a left-over,

6

an undesirable, if she reached the age of twenty-one without a husband), she bore a numerous progeny with little cessation from her multitudinous women's tasks. It was no task for weaklings and developed a type of citizen with distinctive qualities, some good and some bad, but a type capable of changing the land from its primitive state to the modern Indiana with its productive farm lands, its numerous factories, its adequate transportation, its parks, its beautiful homes with beautified grounds, its schools, and its churches—a modern state in a modern world. It bred a race impatient of restraint, resourceful to meet emergencies, self-confident and self-reliant, full of endurance, meditative, religious, optimistic, courageous, industrious, and inventive. The presence of this type of citizen with varied interests was one of the influences into which Wendell Willkie was born.

When the early settlers reached this section of Indiana, it was not only thickly wooded, it was swampy. The long-accumulated and decayed vegetation had enriched the soil so that, according to the survey of the Federal agents under the recent agricultural provisions, it is rated the second most productive farmland in the nation. At this late day, we are prone to criticize the settlers for their, as we say, ruthless destruction of the magnificent forests. They cut down the trees, piled the logs and brush into huge piles, and burned them. We must remember however, that only so could sunlight be let into the gloomy acres and only so could the land be made habitable. After the higher spots were cultivated, there remained the gigantic task of draining the lowlands. These were the homes of swarms of mosquitoes, which the settlers looked upon as fearful annoyances but which modern science tells us were responsible for the dreaded fever and ague—malaria—which plagued the settlers.

The Modern Scene

It is a far cry from the conditions these settlers faced and the modern scene. Today the area is threaded by paved highways, railroads, and electric wires giving, at the touch of a finger, instantaneous light adequate to every need and telephone and telegraph communication with all parts of the world. Wire-fenced fields stretch out as far as the eye can see—fields of corn, of wheat, and of oats. These the pioneer might have seen in small patches, but today the tourist sees along the way what would have been a curiosity to the pioneer—fields of soy beans, fields of clover and alfalfa, fields of tomatoes. All of the crops he did raise have been improved beyond his greatest expectation—if by chance he did hope for better varieties.

One of the greatest improvements of this kind has been in the varieties of corn. Since the discovery of the superiority of hybrid corn, its production has become an important activity in the area surrounding Elwood.

The livestock in this area also would astonish the old settler, not only by its quantity, but by its quality. Improved breeds of cattle and hogs would look almost like new species placed beside the nondescript animals which ran half-wild on the untilled acres. Elwood has stockyards from which large quantities of live stock are shipped direct to packers without passing through the terminal yards elsewhere, although some livestock goes to the terminal markets at Indianapolis.

A growing tendency of late years is the feeding of Western lambs for the market. This, and the production of hogs, is the natural result of the large production of feed grains in this district.

While the automobile has greatly reduced the demand for horses, this area still finds the production of percheron horses not unprofitable. These, of course, have never been produced in the same numbers as meat animals.

Cows, chickens, turkeys, and other farm animals for home consumption are produced. The surplus produce from these is sold to near-by local markets, several cheese factories having been erected in neighboring towns.

"The Modern Miracle"

Undoubtedly the most marvelous change that has taken place in agriculture has been the result of the miracle which is so common that it seems no miracle. Like the seven-year-old who answered her mother's remark about the marvel that she could sit in her home in Elwood and talk to her husband in San Francisco, "Why, Mother, that's because you have a telephone!" we are prone to say, in regard to our ability to eat corn, peas, tomatoes, and other vegetables and fruits at any season and at any place more easily than if they were growing in our back yards, "Oh, that's because we have tin cans!" True enough, but who ever dreamed that the discovery of tinplating and Pasteur's discoveries of bacteria and of the effects of pasteurization would so profoundly affect the diet of the world? So came about the modern miracle of canned foods, which has been one of the most important influences in modern life.

As will be seen, Elwood played a prominent part in the production of this miracle; so it is natural that, given the industrial facilities here, the climate, and the soil, the production of crops for canneries should engage the attention of the farmers. There are in Elwood and a radius of ten miles 57 canning factories. The chief product canned here is the tomato.

Indiana plants 65,000 acres annually to tomatoes, 30 per cent more than any other state in the Union, and produces 350,000 tons of tomatoes each year. The state packs 3,000,000 cases of canned tomatoes, 3,000,000 cases of catsup and chili sauce, 3,000,000 cases of tomato juice, and 1,000,000 cases of tomato puree annually. The territory surrounding Elwood produces about 43 per cent of the tomatoes and tomato products produced in the state. The motto of the Elwood area, both growers and packers, is "Indiana tomatoes excel"; and they are continually striving to improve both the tomato and the method of packing it.

This crop has become so important that the city instituted in 1937 the Annual Tomato Festival. Charles F. Rutledge, who had been working on the plan to secure a highway from Indianapolis to Fort Wayne passing through Elwood and so not only relieve the traffic on other highways and give Elwood a direct route to the state's two largest cities but also acquaint people with

School Where Herman Willkie Taught

Elwood in Willkie's Boyhood

Elwood, proposed the idea to the mayor and a number of other members of a committee which had met to consider the plans for securing the highway. He pointed out that there were fifty-three canning factories which received their mail through the Elwood post office and that the tomatoes grown in the environs of Elwood were famous for their flavor and body.

The idea grew and was a success from the start. As a result of local contests, candidates from Elwood and fifteen neighboring towns and cities competed for the honor of being crowned Tomato Queen on this occasion. In the morning, tours of the canneries and of the Continental Can Company were taken by the huge throngs who visited the city, throngs estimated at 30,000. At 1:30 there was a parade about three miles long. Over fifty floats representing various Elwood industries, business houses, and civic and church organizations extended almost a mile. Large numbers of bicyclists with their bicycles ingeniously and artistically decorated took part in the parade. There was a competition of American Legion drum and bugle corps. The chief address was given by Governor M. Clifford Townsend, and the Tomato Queen was crowned by President Elliott of Purdue University. This was followed by a daylight fireworks display at Callaway Park, a band concert, and then a magnificent night display of aerial fireworks. The day ended with a dance in the armory. Representatives from almost every city in Indiana swelled the attendance. The success of this first festival has been repeated annually since.

This year (1940), contests for the honor of Tomato Queen were held as far away as Paoli and Shelbyville. The queen and the other five finalists were given a three-day visit to Chicago. The festival included inspections of tomato fields and field and canning machinery. Demonstrations were held at various fields. The queen was crowned in the high school gymnasium by President Elliott of Purdue after an address by Governor Townsend. A doll contest, a pillow fight, a pie eating contest, a chicken chase, a pet parade, and numerous other contests for children added to the gaiety offered by the street carnival. On the last day of the three-day festical, a great parade and mass float parade was held. A 600-piece band furnished music. A water carnival and a bathing beauty contest were held at Callaway Park, and the festival closed with the Queen's Ball at the armory.

Developing from the activity in agriculture and its importance grew the Elwood Driving Park and Fair Association, which was organized October 3, 1895. Grounds were purchased about a mile and a half northeast of Elwood and fairs and races were held annually. The importance of the county fairs at this time was due to a number of factors. The real occasion for the fairs, of course, was the growing interest in scientific agriculture and the desire to show what proper care of crops and stock could do. Many farmers saw there for the first time the effect of proper choice of seed, proper tillage, and spraying. There for the first time many of them realized the difference between well-bred live stock and indifferently-bred stock. Their pride was touched, and the fairs did great service by encouraging better farm procedure. The farmers whose products won liberal prizes were well rewarded not only with money but also with pride and satisfaction. The women also had abundant opportunity to show their skill in making butter, cheese, jelly, cake, bread, quilts, and garments.

Here, too, they were able to see exhibited all kinds of farm machinery and to talk them over with representatives of the manufacturers and with each other. Money was usually too scarce with the farmer for him to throw it away on "new-fangled" machines unless he was convinced that they would be profitable.

But another great attraction of the fairs was the excitement in lives often narrow in opportunities. The excitement of the horse races was no less a pleasure to them than it is today to the throngs that crowd Church-hill Downs, Hawthorne, Pimlico, Santa Anita, and Saratoga. Then there were the free shows, the balloon ascension, and the side shows. Just to watch the merry-go-round was enough to keep a country boy happy for half a day, and to ride it was a thrill never to be forgotten. Anyone who has visited a world's fair and seen the attention the crowds give to such amusements as these will have no trouble understanding why these fairs were popular.

Above all, however, was the opportunity to see friends who had not been seen for a long time, for everyone went to the fair. It came at a season when farmwork was light and the days still fairly long. The society which had been almost impossible while the crops were being planted, tended, and harvested was now keenly desired; and here was an opportunity to satisfy that desire. Families took picnic dinners and joined with friends to make these days long-remembered events. This is another custom which the automobile has brought to an end. It is easier now to go twenty miles in an automobile than it was to go five miles with a horse and buggy on good roads. Consequently, one of the chief attractions of the county fair is no more. It has been several years since the Elwood Fair Association ceased to function.

FIRST SETTLER

But the possibility of such achievements was not in the minds of the first settlers. Probably the first permanent settler in Pipe Creek Township (named after the Delaware chief Hopocan—"Tobacco Pipe"), Madison County, Indiana, was Joseph Schell in 1830, who established his home near what is now the southern border of the township. That this was a true wilderness is evident from the following incidents which occurred in this approximate area. On his way to help a neighbor ("Neighbors" were often miles apart), a settler met a bear. He shot it and, as he thought, killed it. After proceeding a short distance, however, he discovered that it had only been wounded and stunned and that it had revived and was following him. He hid behind a tree, knocked it over the head, and killed it with his knife. He hung the carcass on a tree and, on his way home, butchered it and took the meat home.

Another settler, on his way with his fiddle to play for a dance at a neighbor's, was attacked by a number of

16

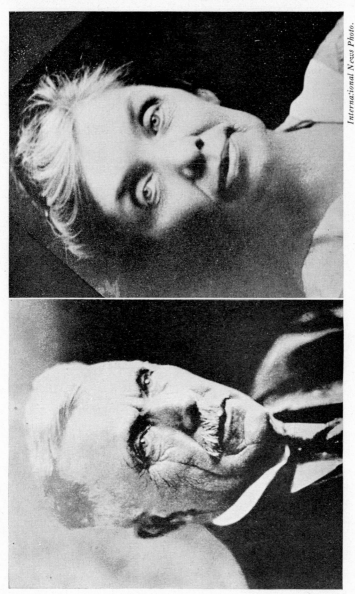

They Devoted Their Lives to Their Children
Mr. and Mrs. Herman F. Willkie

A Pen Reproduction of Willkie's Birthplace

wolves. He found refuge on the roof of an abandoned low log cabin. The wolves made the night hideous with their yelping and kept trying to leap to the roof. Finally, he decided to try the power of music upon the savage beasts. This, or their weariness, quieted them; and he continued to play to his savage audience until day break, when they dispersed.

TRANSPORTATION

Unless the region was to grow up into a number of relatively isolated communities, each economically and politically independent, a system of transportation was essential. Since Indiana had become a state on December 11, 1816, it was impossible for the communities to maintain such isolation. The first roads, of course, were little more than paths widened by the ax. Some of these roads were made by military expeditions. Just how deep mud can be when the February thaw comes is something that the youth of today does not know, but even empty wagons could be moved only with great difficulty and at only a snail's pace when the "bottom fell out" of the roads.

An unverified story which may be slightly exaggerated was current in Illinois where the traffic situation was identical with that about Elwood at this time. The story recites that, as a man was making his slow way along the tortuous rail fence, he became conscious that a man's hat was proceeding along the road almost as fast as he was. Wondering how the hat was being propelled, he pulled up a long stalk of ironweed and cautiously lifted one side of the hat.   To his amazement, he found that he had uncovered a man's head.

"Well," he exclaimed when his astonishment permitted him to speak, "you're certainly in deep!"

"I'll say I am," the man replied; "I'm standing on a load of hay."

Making due allowances for the pioneer tendency to exaggeration, this gives, nevertheless, a vivid idea of the condition of the roads in the early days.

Even as late as 1892, it was all a team could do to pull two-wheeled carts (the front wheels of farm wagons hitched to the wagon tongues) through the streets of Elwood at such times, the wheels sinking so deep that the axles scraped the ground.   Traffic through the mud in the fall made the roads almost impassable when cold weather came in, for the mud froze into such sharp shapes that horses could not safely traverse the roads. Traffic was then generally on horseback along the fences, where the sod had not been churned up by the preceding traffic.   Or course, when a heavy snow came, sleds wore down the sharp roads; and the roads were again passable until a thaw came.   Such conditions compelled the early inhabitants to find amusement and occupation at home during the winter months, for neighbors were far apart, with long periods of complete isolation; today resources for self-entertainment seem to have disappeared, and the radio has put every home in instant touch with the whole world.

The first organized attempt to meet this need for adequate transportation was the formation of companies to build turnpikes, the companies to be reimbursed for their expenditures through tolls. Pipe Creek Township, however, being sparsely settled on account of the extensive marshland, did not seem to these promoters a profitable field for a turnpike. Turnpikes came to Anderson, Alexandria, Frankton, Strawtown, and other surrounding towns; but Pipe Creek Township was left dependent upon local efforts for securing outlets to the outside world. These efforts took the form of corduroy roads—roads made by laying logs side by side across the road. Self-contained as farms were in those days, they needed to go to these towns and villages only occasionally for supplies which they could not themselves produce or make and to take their surplus products to market. Consequently, until long after Elwood became settled, the lack of good roads caused little hardship to the Pipe Creekers in this region. It was not until 1877 that a gravel pike was built from Frankton to Elwood.

When need for easier communications did arise, good township roads were constructed to join Elwood to these improved gravel turnpikes, which became free gravel roads as a result of their purchase by the county about 1900. With the advent of the automobile and the subsequent increase of road traffic, roads were widened and paved, until now Elwood has three paved outlets, giving free and easy access to the network of paved roads that covers our nation.

The advent of the railroads were much more important at the time than good roads would have been. The roads were useful only for horse-borne traffic; the railroads gave speed and made distant travel easy. The first railroad to enter Elwood was the Newcastle & Richmond Railroad, the first train arriving on July 3, 1856. Elwood then was an insignificant village of probably 300 inhabitants, but it was on the route between Richmond and Logansport and so received the benefit of the new road. This road became a part of the Cincinnati & Chicago Airline Railroad and then of the Chicago & Great Eastern Railroad, which became part of the consolidation into the Pennsylvania Railroad Company in 1867. At present it has over three miles of through track and more than double that amount of siding within the limits of Elwood.

The station was built on a platform and was entirely surrounded by water the year round, the station master being compelled to walk from the station to the train on a log to get the mail; and, of course, passengers had to use the log to enter or leave the train.

The Lake Erie & Western Railroad built between Lafayette and Muncie, Indiana, entered Elwood in 1872. It was absorbed by the New York, Chicago, and St. Louis Railroad, popularly known as the Nickel Plate Railroad, in 1922. This railroad now has two miles of through trackage within Elwood and about five miles of siding.

Until railroads could make connections with the mines, the use of coal for railroad locomotives was impossible. However, the railroads passed through vast tracts of virgin forests; and cutting crews were employed to cut wood and cord it along the right-of-way. Sometimes farmers contracted to perform this service. Whenever the supply of wood in the tenders ran low, the train would stop while the crew loaded on a new supply. Fortunately, no one was in a hurry in those days; and it was probably a relief to the passengers to relax from the strain of the tremendous speed of fifteen or twenty miles an hour.

The passenger coaches were made of wood and had open platforms. The link-and-pin coupling bars were operated by hand, as were the brakes, the Westinghouse air brakes not being used anywhere on passenger trains until 1868 nor on freight trains until 1887. It was necessary for the brakeman to run along the tops of the cars to set and release the brakes, a dangerous procedure in wet weather.

The trains were heated by stoves and lighted by oil lamps. Ventilation was simple—through open windows.

Thirty years later, the first interurban car came through Elwood. During that time, the population had increased almost one hundred per cent (of its population when the Lake Erie & Western came) a year. From Indianapolis, a great network of interurban lines was extending throughout the state, making that city the interurban capital of the country. A line already ran from Indianapolis, through Tipton. A line to Elwood was built from Alexandria in 1899, and later extended to Tipton. The citizens of Elwood had been promised that the line would be completed about the middle of the year, but it was not till the very last day of 1902 that the first car went from Elwood to Tipton, making the trip of twelve miles in forty minutes. Both the entry of this car to Elwood and its departure were witnessed by a huge crowd, and the car was jammed with passengers. January 3, 1901, the line from Indianapolis to Anderson was opened and later extended to Muncie and Fort Wayne. Another line was built from Anderson through Alexandria to Wabash.

With the increase of automobile traffic, however, the line ceased to be profitable. Passenger trains were discontinued June 30, 1931; and freight service was discontinued October 15, 1931. The interurban line had taken over the street car line; but that had been discontinued a few years before this, cross-city transportation being given by the interurban cars.

When the interurban lines were discontinued, the Indiana Traction Company deeded its station building to the city (September 21, 1931) in consideration of being relieved of the expense and responsibility of taking up the tracks. This building is across Main Street from the City Hall and now contains the office of the City Water Works, and two retail stores.

Of the great interurban empire that once spread its network across Indiana, only the Indianapolis-Seymour line will operate from Indianapolis by the end of the summer, the line to Fort Wayne and the branch line from Muncie to Newcastle being now in process of substituting bus and truck service for the electric service.

Three bus lines now give Elwood the connections formerly given by the interurbans. The line from Muncie to Kokomo gives transportation each way eight times daily. The line from Indianapolis makes three trips each way, and the one from Anderson makes the round trip four times daily.

But, in 1830, fourteen years after Indiana had been admitted to the Union as a state, these developments were not even imagined. It is probable that few knew that Joseph Schell had settled in the region. The population increased, roads of a sort connected these farmers with the stores and markets at Anderson, Frankton, Strawtown, Lapel, Alexandria, Pendleton, Tipton, and other towns within the radius of a day's drive in the summer, when the roads were firm and fairly smooth. The first schoolhouse in the township was built in 1838, the first mill (to grind cornmeal) was erected in 1839 or 1840, and a sawmill was constructed near Frankton about the same time. Slowly, almost imperceptibly, the region was passing out of the pioneer stage.

COUNTRY STORE

But Elwood had not yet been born. That event occurred in 1852, when William Barton opened a general store at a crossing of roads. Picture a general store of that time. It was the prototype of the department store of today, but vastly different. A crude building with a rough board counter on one side and shelves on both sides and across the back. Barrels of sugar, crackers, vinegar, and salt, bags of beans and rice, boxes of strong and odorous soap, bins for coffee, tin cans for tea and a few spices, rolls of calico and muslin, kegs of nails, ax and adz heads, scythe blades and snathes, boxes of tobacco, pails of hard cheap candies. The simple requirements of a raw community were scattered higgledy-piggledy about the one room, but not in such con-

25

fusion that the store-keeper could not find anything in his stock.

About the stove near the center of the store were a number of empty nail kegs, where on rainy days and in winter the farmers sat, sawdust-filled tobacco boxes convenient for the tobacco chewers' marksmanship, discussing. What? The weather (for the weather was important for their crops) their farms, hunting, fishing, the "goin's on" of their neighbors (a mile or so away) the schools, the churches, and (above all) politics. The last was a matter of direct importance to these country store "loafers", as they are often called by people who do not consider themselves loafers when they read the newspapers and magazines, attend a picture show or a lecture or a political convention, or travel a hundred— or even a thousand—miles to interview a man for a quarter of an hour. This was the early farmers' forum. Here they learned the give and take of argument, the possibilities of logic.

But to return to their interest in politics: They had no great interest in what was going on in Washington. It was too far away, newspapers were rare, and the influence of the government upon them was one chiefly of "salutary neglect". They had more interest in the state government. Some of the farmers had been to Indianapolis; they perhaps knew their state representatives personally or, at least, had heard them speak; and the influence of the state government was more distinctly felt. Their chief interest, however, was in local government. Then as now, taxes were a matter of direct concern. They knew the board of trustees

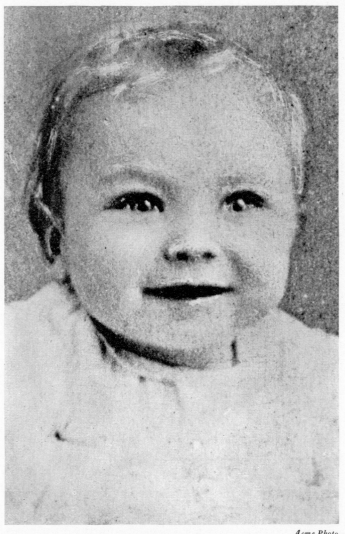

Wendell Willkie at Six Months

First Methodist Church

Lewellyn

Episcopal Church
Where Willkie Worshiped at Elwood

of their townships; some of them had been on the board, and some of them had wanted to be on it. The affairs of the county were their affairs.

Politics, therefore, and especially local politics, were of perennial interest to the early Indianian and to no one more than to these rough-looking country store "loafers." This was no less true of the community about Elwood than of other parts of Indiana; and, as will appear, the Willkies, from their first arrival in Elwood, became intensely interested in politics—or, if you prefer the term, government. Wendell Willkie could not have lived in Elwood, could not have been a member of his family, without having heard politics from the time of his earliest memories—not the abstractions of politics, but the practical phases of politics and government. That is not to say that he, nor the mass of citizens of Elwood, were professionally interested in politics, merely that an interest in the functioning of government is an inheritance from the forums of the country store.

Behind the store, or perhaps in separate buildings, would be appropriate pens and storage space for the furs, chickens, turkeys, ducks, pigs, calves, grain, and hay which the farmer might bring in payment for his purchases. These products would then be taken by the storekeeper to the larger communities when the roads permitted. There were no set prices either for the storekeeper's goods nor for the articles which he took in exchange. Consequently, the country people developed great shrewdness in bargaining, in which they took great delight.

ELWOOD BORN

The territory about Barton's store had been surveyed (1819-1824) under the general land survey authorized by the Federal government at the time the Northwest Territory was organized. The year following the establishment of this store, James Anderson, Mark Simmons, and J. B. Frazier laid out a town, which they called Quincy. Three east and west streets were laid out, Simmons Street (now South A Street), Main Street (still known by that name) and Walnut Street (now North A Street). The one north and south street was and is known as Anderson Street. The original town plot shows six lots north and twelve lots south of Main Street.

When application was made to make Quincy a postoffice, it was discovered that there was already a Quincy in Spencer County. The town continued to be called Quincy, although the postoffice was known as Duck Creek, because the region was a duck swamp much frequented by hunters. This situation was confusing and unsatisfactory in general. There was considerable discussion about a suitable name. There was an attempt to use the name of some of the more prominent inhabitants, but modesty and sometimes jealousy raised objection. Finally, someone pointing to Mr. Frazier's six-year-old son, said "Why not name it for Elwood?" And so it was agreed. The town assumed the name of Elwood, July 21, 1869.

The first person born in Elwood seems, according to the investigations of the Elwood Historical Society, to have been Florence Burress, daughter of Solomon A. and Margaret Burress, who moved to Quincy in 1857.

Florence was born on May 9, 1858, on the site of the present senior high school. Her granddaughter, Mrs. G. T. Hasecuster resides now at South L and 16th Streets, Elwood.

DOCTORS

As has been said, Elwood was swampy and therefore far from a healthful place to live. The pioneers were a hardy people; but doctors found a strenuous, if not always remunerative, life. The practice of medicine was very simple in those days. Almost nothing was known of the causes of disease, almost none of the modern physicians' and surgeons' tools had been invented, chemistry was in its infancy, and bacteriology had barely begun in Europe. The regular procedure for an aspiring doctor was to associate himself with some practicing physician, generally an old man; observe him and assist him; and, if possible, attend lectures given by physicians in the community. Then, when he felt qualified to strike out for himself, he secured a room for an office, hung up his shingle, and began to practice for himself.

That doctors so trained were a great help is unquestionable, even though they were ignorant of most that a graduate from a medical school today has learned. They did know something about human suffering, were men of sympathy, were able to give relief in many cases, understood first-aid, and accomplished much that mere medical knowledge secured from text-books is even yet unable to accomplish. Most of these early doctors were conscientious practitioners. They would go to a patient whenever called, day or night, fair or storm, riding

31

through mud knee deep to their horses, or traveling distances of fifteen or twenty miles over frozen ground in bitter cold. The fevers and chills resulting from the presence of swamps required enormous quantities of quinine, still the only efficient remedy for malaria. Since then, clearings and ditches have removed the stagnant surface water in the community and the decaying vegetation has dried up and been burned or plowed under. Consequently, fever and ague have disappeared.

The first doctor to settle in Elwood was Dr. Robert Douglass. Dr. J. M. DeHority, whose family has played an important part in Elwood history, came next, while Elwood was still known as Quincy.

Churches

Even preceding the physician to the body came the physician to the spirit. About 1848, a Methodist preacher on the Anderson circuit came to the neighborhood of the present Elwood and preached in a private home. The attendants organized the First Methodist Episcopal church, the first religious society in Duck Creek, now Elwood. This church erected its first building in 1854, the year after the town was laid out, on the site of the present fine First Methodist Church building.

As with doctors, the minister's remuneration was more largely in satisfaction than in worldly goods, although he did receive from his parishioners contributions of food. Most, if not all, of the early ministers in the country districts, however, had other occupations. Some were blacksmiths, some carpenters, some farmers, etc.

Julia and Charlotte Willkie

Wendell Willkie in 1906

A church of the Christian denomination was organized in Elwood in 1852 and built a house of worship a few years later. In 1866, the Catholic parish at Anderson sent two priests to minister to a mission at Elwood. Later a priest came periodically from Anderson; and, by 1880, the congregation had become too large to be accommodated in a residence; and a brick church was constructed. Besides the churches more specifically mentioned, Elwood has the Grace Methodist Church (organized in 1865), a Presbyterian church (organized May 8, 1880), the Pilgrim Holiness Church (organized in 1895), a United Brethren church (organized in 1900) a Wesleyan Methodist church (organized in 1906), a Pentacostal Assembly Church (organized in 1914), a Nazarene church (organized in May, 1917), an Episcopal church (organized in 1903), the First Church of Christ Scientist (organized March 30, 1899), and a Lutheran church (organized in 1893).

Schools

The same interest in education which prompted the framers of the Articles of Confederation to specify that Section 16 of each township of 36 sections should be devoted to school purposes prompted the early settlers to take an interest in education. The earliest schools were taught by traveling schoolmasters, some of whom had no qualifications to teach. Many of the teachers, however, who used this means of maintaining themselves and of securing some funds to assist them in completing their education or in eking out a scanty living in some other occupation were not only conscientious but competent men. Since the children were needed to plant and to harvest the crops, the school terms had to be accommodated to the local situations. The schoolmasters boarded around, as is so vividly described in Eggleston's *Hoosier Schoolmaster*, and often took their pay in coon skins and other articles which they were able to sell.

The schools became the center of one of the outstanding entertainments of the early inhabitants of the Middle West—the spelling bee. This was essentially a social gathering, for almost everyone in the community and in the neighboring communities attended, as they did the revival meetings held in the spring when the ground was too soft to permit of work in the fields. The spelling matches were the climax of these gatherings. Schools prided themselves on having champion spellers and championship teams, who would attend spelling bees in other communities and try to bring home the honors. Webster's blue-back spellers, the forerunners of the Webster dictionary, were the source of the spelling words. In those days, spelling words were chosen for their difficulty rather than their usability. The good spellers adopted the simple procedure of learning the spelling book by heart. At a spelling bee in 1911, in which the words were taken from this blue-back speller, a man, who studied it probably forty years before, was able frequently to stop me as I gave out the words, and announce what the next word was. The words were spelled by syllables, the word being pronounced to the end of each syllable at the conclusion of each.

The first school in this community was built just outside the present limits of the city, on what was then known as the Carlisle Derry farm. This was in 1852. Plank desks and benches were used. Another log school was constructed at what is now the intersection of South P and Anderson Streets. After the town was laid out, in 1853, a school was opened in the old Christian church, at the present 1416 West Main Street. It was then transferred to the old Methodist Episcopal church at the site of the present building. In 1856, a log school was erected at Red Corner, two miles east of the present Elwood. The windows were formed by cutting out sections of the logs and covering the openings with greased paper.

The first permanent school building in Elwood was the present two-story frame building at 1623 East Main Street. The first brick school, at the site of the present Central Building, was constructed in 1875. It consisted of four rooms, and four more were added in 1881. Other schools were built as the population increased. The present Central Building was constructed in 1897.

In 1888, Herman F. Willkie, father of Wendell Willkie, became superintendent of schools in Elwood and organized a high school course. He himself taught algebra, arithmetic, and Latin. The other subjects of the two-year course were taught by Daniel King. After two years, the high school had an enrollment of 42; and Mr. Willkie's successor taught all the classes. He left the school on its honor an hour each day so that he might supervise the seven grade rooms. About a month after this system was inaugurated, a boy waited for the superintendent after dismissal to confess that he had brought an apple to school, cut it up, and passed it around; but not a student would eat it. The apple, the pupil went on to say, was thrown into the waste basket. The high school secured its commission in 1892, the year that the tin plate mill opened. In 1891, the course was enlarged to a three-year course; and, in 1893, the Elwood High School began to give a full four-year course. The high school work started in the old building, was taken to the Linwood Building in 1892, to the Odd Fellows' hall in 1898, and to the Central Building in 1899. In 1915, the present senior high school was built; and a large addition was made in 1933. The present gymnasium, built in 1936, seats 2,500 for an athletic contest. By placing seats on the playing floor, over seven hundred more can be seated. When the excavation was being made, vats from an old tanyard which was there in the 1870's were unearthed. The present grade schools are Central, Osborn, Washington, Linwood, and Edgewood. An idea of the need for these schools may be seen from the growth of the population. In 1874, there were 400 people in Elwood; in 1889, there were 15,289. Since then, the population has declined to its present 10,918. Above the main entrance to the Central Building, in which Wendell Willkie attended high school, the builders inscribed the prophetic words THE HOPE OF OUR COUNTRY. Here, Mr. Willkie will greet his former schoolmates and make a few remarks before he goes to Callaway Park to make his speech of acceptance of the Republican nomination for the presidency of the United States.

Besides the public schools, Elwood has one parochial school—the Saint Joseph Parochial School. This was opened in a small one-room frame building September 8, 1892, with a single teacher. It has grown until, in addition to the grade school work, it gives two years of state-accredited high school work. It now occupies the building constructed in 1911. It is used as a training school for the Sisters of Saint Joseph who are studying in the Saint Joseph Academy at Tipton, Indiana, twelve miles away, to become teachers.

Naturally many other changes accompanied these. In 1870 William Barton, who had established the first store eighteen years earlier, opened the first bank and built the first grain elevator, clear evidence, not only of his own prosperity, but of the growth of the rural community and its agricultural and economic prosperity, for the population of the town itself was less than 400. A report for 1874 comments upon the large shipments of lumber, particularly heading and stave material from Elwood. Besides the Methodist and Christian churches, there was a brick schoolhouse, a railroad depot, a good hotel, a livery stable, a tanyard, a flour mill, three druggists, a harness maker, four shoemakers, and two blacksmiths, a remarkable number of establishments for so small a community. It must be remembered, however, that people did not travel twenty, a hundred, or two hundred miles to do their shopping, so that these firms could count upon the patronage of all the area within several miles' radius.

NEWSPAPERS

A few years later, in 1877, the first newspaper, the Elwood *Review*, was established; but it soon died. In 1880, another paper, The Elwood *Free Press* began publication.   The Elwood *Review* (assuming the name of the first paper) began in 1888 and was consolidated with the *Free Press* and was made a daily in 1892.   It changed hands and was published as the Elwood *Press* every Thursday and as the *Record* every afternoon until 1922, when both papers were suspended.   In the meantime, the Elwood *Leader* and the Elwood *Daily Call* had been founded in 1891.   These two papers consolidated in 1894 and are still published as the Elwood *Call-Leader*.

It is the custom among some to sneer at the early country newspapers, contrasting them with the metro-politan papers.   That, however, is just as sensible as to sneer at a garden hoe because it is not an American Beauty rose.   These papers filled a definite need.   They were eagerly awaited by their subscribers, who had little in-terest in what might be happening to some actor, or politician, or merchant in New York or Chicago but had a very lively interest in their neighbors and in their friends, who as a rule lived within the area reported by the local newspaper.   Poor letter writers as these people generally were, the weekly paper was essentially a round robin of news.   Is it any worse to be interested in the private life of people one knows than to be interested in the private life of utter strangers?

As the community became urbanized, the newspapers assumed more and more the function of the city paper. while still giving primary attention to Elwood and Pipe Creek Township, the Call-Leader does not neglect state, national, and international news.   In other words, the character of the newspapers published in Elwood has been fitted constantly to the requirements of its readers. Incidentally, the whole nation is now very much concerned with news about Elwood, its citizens, and its history. Hardly a day has passed since the twenty-eighth of June that some of the minor happenings of Elwood, both now and in the past, have not appeared in city dailies from New York to San Francisco. Local news has become national news.

So the history of Elwood moved along unmomentously, except for its own citizens, for births and deaths, weddings and christenings, new homes and occasions for hospitality are momentous to rich and poor wherever they may be. A change here and there, the opening of the first factory in Elwood, a flax factory, employing about fifty people, opened by Captain John H. Wagner and Milton Kidwell and operated until jute was imported to make tow for ropes (The building burned in 1881); a new school—events moved along casually until the volcanic year of 1887. At least, this year disrupted all the life of Elwood and remade it. Agriculture ceased to be its chief interest and dependence, and industry took the town by the hand.

Gas

Two conditions separated by great geologic ages combined to bring about this change. When this region had been deep undersea, the steady deposit of the shells of microscopic sea animals had laid down great layers that had been pressed into limestone, covering immense layers of vegetable matter which had, by some cataclysm of nature been sunk below the level of the sea. In some places, this had resulted in great deposits of coal; here it had resulted in great reservoirs of gas. Several layers of stone had imprisoned this gas, but the Trenton limestone is the most porous and, in Indiana, contained great stores of gas. A booklet put out in 1893 to celebrate the opportunities of Elwood says, "The fact that the Indiana gas field lies upon the crown of what is known to geologists as the 'Cincinnati arch of Trenton limestone' makes it as well assured as any speculative theory can ever be that the gas reservoir beneath us is practically illimitable and beyond the scope of computation."

Elwood and its environs were not alone in the faith that the gas reservoir was "practically illimitable." When gas was discovered near Elwood in 1887, just as everywhere else in those days of faith in the illimitability of natural resources, immense quantities of the precious gas were wasted. Huge flaming torches were set up, flaming day and night to advertise the presence of this new fuel which required only a pipe line to supply heat and light without further effort. In yard after yard and at street corners, the gas was left burning because it was too much trouble to shut it off at bedtime or in the morning or too expensive to have that done. Many wells were allowed to burn for weeks before any attempt was made to cap them, merely because it was not convenient to cap them sooner. For five years, this unforgivable waste went on. Then sanity dawned, and the gas waste was checked.

But, while it lasted, the gas brought to Elwood great numbers of people, great quantities of capital, new industries, a new way of living, new outlooks. Between 1877 and 1887, the year gas was discovered in the community, the population increased about 105%. In the next three years, the population increased about 300%, to 2,229. Three years later, the population was 9,031. One result of this increase was that Elwood, which was laid out in 1852 and incorporated as a town in 1872 with a population of less than 400, was incorporated as a city in 1891 with a population growing past the three thousand mark by leaps. William A. DeHority, still an active citizen and a storehouse of local history, was the first mayor.

Gas mains were laid through the streets; and street lights were set up, mere flambeaux burning in the open air. This was a great improvement, of course, over the unlighted streets; but the lights were not brilliant. Later, gauze mantles surrounded by chimneys were installed; but still they were not satisfactory. About time the movement for the incorporation as a city was under way, agitation for the construction of an electric light plant arose. There were many who thought that gas was the more desirable for lighting, but the advocates of electricity won out.

ELECTRICITY

There was a great celebration on the day that the electric light plant was to open. A band marched up and down the streets; and, at two o'clock on the afternoon of August 1, 1891, the mayor's small son pulled the throttle that put into motion the machinery for the plant. This plant was opened by the Elwood Electric Light Plant and was taken over by the Elwood Electric Street Railway in 1893, when that company began operations. When the Union Traction Company took over the street railway, it did not buy the light plant, which was ultimately purchased by the Indiana General Service Company, which now operates it.

Electricity was at once used for street lighting, but it came into use slowly for home lighting. Many homes had put in gas, and it was no small task to take out the gas fixtures and replace them with electric fixtures. Besides, the gas rates were ridiculously low. No meters were attached to the gas lines. A flat rate of ten cents a month was charged for the use of gas for cooking, seventy-five cents a month for its use for heating, and five cents a month for each jumbo light in the house. At these rates, the consumer was permitted to use as much gas as he wished; and some found it more economical to let the gas burn continuously than to buy matches. Naturally, they hesitated to change over to electricity.

Gas Failure

It is easy to imagine the consternation of the people in the south part of Elwood when, on the morning of January 20, 1903, they found that they had no gas. It was a very cold morning; and they had no gas for cooking, heating, nor light. What had happened? Early that morning, the gas regulator house on the south end of the city had caught fire. The fire department soon put the blaze out, but it took a few hours to make repairs so that the service could be resumed. One tradition says that there was a complete shutdown throughout the city, but the newspaper report the next day completely refutes this tradition.

The tradition, however, persists that the gas supply ceased suddenly. What actually happened is much less dramatic. Pumping stations had been put in to pump gas to Fort Wayne, Chicago, and Indianapolis. As a result, the gas reserve was reduced, the pressure was lowered, and water began to enter the wells. The handwriting on the wall became visible and intelligible to all. On November 1, 1901, the superintendent of one of the gas lines was tried for wasting gas. The factories, which had leased large acreages and constructed their own pipe lines, finding the pressure steadily reduced, began to supplement their gas with coal. The Pennsylvania Railroad Company announced that, in the event of the failure of the gas supply, it was prepared to ship in coal at a very low rate, for the freight business of around $200,000 a year from each of a number of the gas towns was too valuable to lose.

As moisture crept into the wells and pipes, the supply on cold days became undependable, especially early in the mornings, as the water would freeze wherever the pipes reached the surface and constrict or completely stop the flow of gas and the pressure was too low to keep the pipes clear. Consequently, housewives might get up some morning and find no gas to cook breakfast with. Thus, Julia Willkie writes in a letter that she remembers the winter the gas failed in the Willkie home and they had to burn newspapers and old furniture in an attempt to keep warm. Others remember cutting wood for fuel.

When the gas pressure dropped too low, the larger factories turned to the use of coal. The houses which had sprung up with the industrial growth of the city

45

had chimneys suitable for gas but not for other fuels; so it would have been a real hardship for the citizens to have been compelled to change fuel suddenly. During cold weather, men were sent out to thaw out the small lines, which were wholly or partly on the surface; and the pipes often had to be thawed out near the houses at the point where they left the earth. As leases expired or were abandoned, the wells became the property of the land-owners, who were able to supply their own needs for many years. Some wells are still sufficiently strong to serve their owners.

In 1912, the gas properties were purchased by the Central Indiana Gas Company. Manufactured gas was piped in from Muncie for some time. At present, an abundant supply of gas from West Virginia and Texas sufficient for both home and industrial needs is piped into Elwood by that company.

Tin Plate

The second influence which smashed to smithereens the old way of living in Elwood was as unintentional as were the geological conditions which created the fuel that brought it about. The most common metal, next to aluminum, is iron; and its uses are too numerous to list. However, it readily rusts when exposed to moist air and so is unsuited for many household uses and lacks permanence in many other uses. Fortunately, a method of coating sheets of iron with tin, which is not affected by ordinary atmospheric conditions, was discovered.

Tin and iron possess mutually opposite characteristics, but iron plates covered with tin possess most of the

46

desirable characteristics of each. Tin is fairly soft; easily flattened; almost without tenacity, so that cold makes it brittle, even powdery. It was found, however, that steel bars, carefully manufactured for the purpose, could be rolled into thin sheets and chemically treated so that a thin coating of tin could be given it. In common speech, such a plated sheet of steel is known as tin.

This tin possesses the tenacity and strength of steel but will not rust. It may be used in almost any way that the uncoated sheets of steel might be used—for roofs and ceilings, for gutters and downspouts, for cups and other containers, for funnels, and for all the other uses so common and so commonly known. By this process, the uses of steel have been multiplied; and tin has become useful for other things than alloys.

At the beginning of the last decade of the Nineteenth Century, a practical monopoly of the production of this product was held by England and Wales. Some iron was mined in Wales, and more was shipped from Spain and Norway; the largest tin mines of Europe are in Cornwall, England; and coal was abundant at home. The process had been perfected there, and the Welsh workers had attained great skill in the work. In order for the United States to secure tin plate, it was necessary to pay freight charges on the iron to Wales and on the finished product across the Atlantic.

Having a monopoly on tin, the English firms felt it to their interest to hold up prices, a tendency of all monopolies. They cut down the working day to eight hours, not in the interest of the workers, as was the case in later years both abroad and in the United States, but to

47

reduce production. It is hard for monopolies to see, as Wendell Willkie and his father have both believed, that it was to the interest of both consumer and producer that production be increased, prices reduced, and consumption encouraged. As in the rubber monopoly of the English, the cotton monopoly of the South, and the nitrate monopoly of Chile, short-sightedness in this direction led to competition and the disruption of the economic life of the countries maintaining the monopolies.

The growing demand for tin in this country, then, made the manufacture of tin in this country highly desirable. This was undertaken as early as 1873 at several points in Ohio and Pennsylvania, but the projects failed. This was partly due to the absence of skilled labor, but chiefly to the fact that the tariff on tin plate was so low that the young industries were unable to meet the costs of imported tin, as their plants were small, the original outlay for plant and machinery was high, production was slow, and wages were higher than abroad.

In the 1880's, William McKinley, Jr., then chairman of the Ways and Means Committee of The House of Representatives, sponsored a tariff bill increasing the tariff on certain manufactured articles. This tariff bill was passed, The McKinley Tariff of 1890; and, among other items, it doubled the tariff on tin, making the duty two and two-tenths cents a pound on the imported article.

Dan G. Reid, having risen from the very lowest position in the Second National Bank of Richmond to the position of cashier and vice-president, and William B. Leeds, superintendent of the Richmond-Logansport Division of the Pennsylvania Railroad, were impressed by the opportunity to get a cheap fuel at Elwood and saw a great future in the manufacture of tin plate in this country. There was abundant iron ore near Pittsburgh; tin in the Black Hills of South Dakota (Most of our tin now comes from the Dutch East Indies); and, between them, an apparently limitless supply of cheap and easily controlled fuel—a perfect combination. So they determined to set up a tin plate mill here.

After making this a success, they became interested in other tin plate mills and were instrumental in the many consolidations which ultimately became the United States Steel Corporation. Mr. Reid was a financier who impressed even the masters of finance in the East; Mr. Leeds was more directly concerned with the production. They never lived in Elwood but commuted back and forth on the railroad from their homes in Richmond. Both became very wealthy, and Mr. Leeds became known as the Tin Plate King of the world.

There has long been a tradition that a large part of a Welsh mill was dismantled and shipped to Elwood and set up here. This is based on a very minor detail. The "pickling" process, the bathing of the steel sheets in sulphuric acid, is very important. A pickling machine was brought here from Wales, but everything else used in the factory was American-made. It was modeled, it is true, after the machines used in the Welsh mills; but the originals were not followed exactly, and improvements were made. The tin mill at Gas City did import several pieces of Welsh machinery, but practically all the mills in this country were completely equipped with American-made machinery.

The first equipment for the tin-plate mill contained four hot mills, Specially made Bessemer steel bars were heated a cherry red in gas furnaces. These were then carried to hot rolls, through which they were passed several times, being doubled, reheated, rerolled, etc., until they were the desired thickness and length and made into a pack of eight thicknesses. These were then cut by shearmen into the desired sizes and passed to openers, who separated the sheets. The sheets were then pickled and then annealed by being placed in ovens, where they remained ten to twelve hours at a very high temperature. After cooling, they were passed through cold rolls singly four times and then annealed once more. When they were removed from the annealing ovens the second time, they were treated with a white pickle, the former being a "black" pickle, to remove impurities.

This left the plates perfectly smooth, in a condition known as black plate. These plates were immersed in a bath of palm oil until all water disappeared, the oil forming a flux for the tin, the first coat of which was then applied in the tin pot. After being washed, these plates were then painted with oil by hand. The last step was to run the plates through rolls running in palm oil (An inferior tin was made in England to compete with American tin by using an acid instead of a palm oil flux) and distribute the second coating of tin smoothly over the plates. The tin was then polished by passing the plates through bran and rubbing them briskly with sheepskin.

Since there were only four hot mills, the other equipment was set up sufficient to take care of only this out-

Duck Creek, Where Willkie Learned to Swim

Herman F. Willkie and the Willkie Boys

put. This was the first plant in America built for the sole purpose of producing tin-plate. There were plants which made tinplate before the erection of this plant; but, with them, the plating of tin was only an addition to other sheet metal work. Moreover, this was the first *successfully operated* tin mill in the country.

In 1892, the year the American Tin Plate Company opened, Grover Cleveland was running for the presidency against President Benjamin Harrison. William McKinley, the sponsor of the tariff bill which had made the erection of the plant feasible, was then governor of Ohio. He was invited to speak at a great "Tin Plate Opening and Grand Republican Rally" on September 13, 1892. The mill had opened in June, but this was considered a fitting time for its dedication. In fact, the mill was not successful when it first opened and almost 300 Welshmen had been imported; and the company was reorganized. The original name had been the American Sheet Tin Plate Company.

Governor McKinley spoke from the balcony of the old opera house—now the Masonic Hall—on Anderson Street between South A and South B Streets. The balcony is no longer there, but the table at which Governor McKinley stood to make his speech is being used as a conference table at the Willkie headquarters, 1113 South Anderson Street, Elwood. The street then was gravel and mud, and the heavy downpour of rain all day had churned it almost into a hogwallow. Nearly every city in Indiana was represented at the opening. Governor Chase of Indiana also spoke, and he held an umbrella over Governor McKinley during his speech. McKinley emphasized the importance of the protective tariff to such industries as the one that was then being dedicated.

About 20,000 are estimated to have attended this rally. Large numbers were escorted through the Tin Plate mills. Farmers who went through the mills wore heavy rubber shoes or boots, on account of the rain and mud. The Welshmen would lead them over the hot iron floor and then have them stand until the soles of their overshoes or boots melted. The workmen enjoyed the joke much more than the farmers, needless to say.

The trademark of the American Tin Plate Company was an American Eagle flying away with the British lion in its talons. This was much more than American braggadocio. We talk much today about the importance to us of affairs across the seas, implying often that this is something new. While the success of the American Tin Plate Company was fortunate for this country, it illustrates just as truly as if it had been tragic how nations are bound together and how incidents thousands of miles away, incidents over which they have no control, may bring disaster. Following the introduction of the manufacture of tin plate in this country, 234 out of approximately 500 English tin plate mills were forced to close. (The term *English mills*, of course, includes those in Wales).

This, of course, was a result of the tariff. Large numbers of workers were imported from Wales. As one of the Welshmen who came to the Elwood plant said recently, the tin workers in Wales said, "Tin plate is done here; we might as well go to America." All the hot mill and tin house men in the local plant, and undoubtedly in many others throughout the country, came from Wales.

One of these immigrants who came over to work in the tin industry was Jim Davis. Because there was a strike in Pittsburgh, where he had been working, he came to Elwood (in a box car for economy's sake) one hot July day in 1893. In 1896, there was a strike at the mills. It is a difficult thing at this late date to discover the precise cause of the strike, but the foreman of the hot mills at the time states that it was due to the attempt of one of the union heads to bring beer into the plant contrary to the rules. He was discharged, and a considerable number of men went on strike out of sympathy with him. Tin plate mills had been opened in Pittsburgh, and some of the foremen had been offered positions there. While the strike was on, a number of the men went to Pittsburgh to look the mills over.

When they got there, they were out of money, not having even enough to buy tobacco. Jim Davis would see some mill men coming and would tell them that he was from Elwood, where there was a strike, and would ask for some tobacco. He was so successful that he was able to supply all the rest with tobacco, too. The strike was over in six weeks, and the men all returned to Elwood.

In 1898, Davis was elected city clerk of Elwood and served till 1902. The City Hall was built during his term of office; and his name is on the corner stone, with that of the other officers of the time. He studied law on the side in the law offices of Greenlee and Call and at times went to the law office of Willkie and Willkie (the father and mother of Wendell Willkie) to borrow books. He was county recorder from 1903 to 1907. From 1921 to 1930, he was secretary of labor under three presidents. Today, he is Senator James J. Davis of Pennsylvania, having risen from heater in the tin mills to some of the highest honors that his fellow citizens can give him.

In a recent letter, he says: "It was a good town for a young man to grow. There were the customary swimming holes that emptied into the west branch of the White River, shaded streets, a quiet, peaceful air in the midst of one of the world's great agricultural areas. Elwood was only a small town of about 12,000 people and we all got to know each other pretty well which is typical of the small towns of that section."

Many improvements in machinery and operation were made in the Elwood plant. One of the foremen, originally from Wales, visited that country in 1910. He found that the same methods were being used in the tin mills there as in 1893, when he came to this country. Numerous changes, however, had been made in the local plant and adopted throughout the tin industry. It was a common thing for one of the older Welshmen to say to someone suggesting a new method, "That's never been tried; it can't be done." When the company was having great difficulty with welded water pipes, one of the workmen suggested a 40-foot template to be used in the welding to avoid mashing in the pipe so as to check the water flow.

Indianapolis Star.

Where Wendell Willkie Attended High School

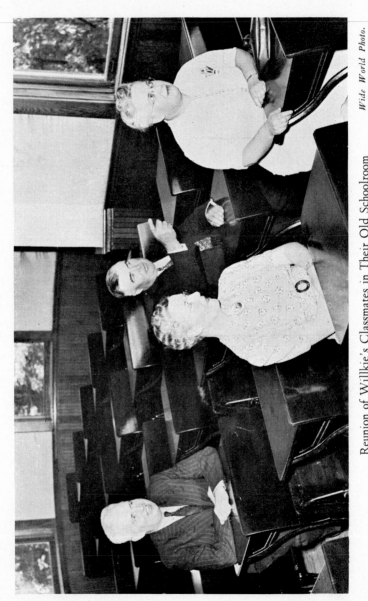

Reunion of Willkie's Classmates in Their Old Schoolroom

"Who ever heard of a 40-foot template?" his foreman asked him.

"What difference does it make what has been heard of?" the workman replied; and, when the foreman was away one day, he made a 40-foot template.

It worked so successfully that a $7,000 pump which had been purchased to force water through the pipes was no longer necessary. It was through improvements such as this resulting from a lack of respect for tradition and from the habit of thinking, which was one of the social heritages left by the pioneers of our land, that the mill was able to grow, improve its product, and increase in efficiency.

When the tin plate mill opened in 1892, the population of Elwood was 5,000. Mills from Montpelier, Anderson, Atlanta, Gas City, Middletown, and other small cities contributed their plants to the Elwood plant. The giant engine moved here from Montpelier was used for years and was commonly known as the Montpelier engine. When the tin plate plant opened, there were in Elwood two banks, the Farmers' Bank, reorganized as the First National Bank, and the Citizens' Exchange Bank. In 1907, the Elwood Trust Company was formed, and the Elwood State Bank was founded. At present, there are three banks: the first National, the Elwood State, and the Citizens' Exchange.

But the success of the tin plate industry was not dependent wholly upon that industry. In the early Nineteenth Century, Napoleon offered a prize of 12,000 francs to any one who could find a way of preserving food for his armies. Nicholas Appert, a Frenchman, discovered the process of canning in 1814, too late to aid Napoleon, but not too late to serve the world. Just why Appert's method was successful (at least partially) was not known. Pasteur, another Frenchman, discovered bacteria; and, in 1895, three years after the establishment of the tin plate mill in Elwood, H. L. Russell, of Wisconsin, and W. L. Underwood and Dr. Prescott, of the Massachusetts Institute of Technology, discovered that the spoilage of canned goods was caused by bacteria from the atmosphere. Knowing the cause, it was a simple thing to discover methods of processing canned goods, so that spoilage is now practically unknown. This has enormously increased the demand for canned goods, and so of tin cans, and so of tin plate. As is mentioned elsewhere, the increase in the demand for canned goods has brought Elwood, not only canning factories, but also a factory to manufacture the cans. The use of tin plate extended to paint cans, food containers, beer cans, oil cans, pails, washing machines, buttons, picture frames, signs, metal ceilings, cream separators, etc., etc.

As a result, the tin plate mills grew. From the four hot mills with which the plant started in 1892, it grew to 10 in 1894, 16 in 1899, and 22 in 1900. Tin plate was shipped to all parts of the United States and to foreign countries. All this meant a similar increase in the number of employees. In 1914, mechanical doublers began to be used and the number of mills was reduced to 9 double and 2 single mills. At the same time, overhead cranes and other mechanical devices had been added.

A number of tin mills have been erected since 1892 in various parts of the United States. Most of these were later merged into the American Sheet & Tin Plate Company, now a subsidiary of the United States Steel Corporation. This merger included the Elwood plant. In 1936, the American Sheet and Tin Plate Company merged with the Carnegie-Illinois Steel Corporation.

Under the control of the United States Steel Corporation, much welfare work was done for the employees. In 1922, an emergency hospital was built; and trained nurses were on duty at all times. A welfare home for women employees was built in 1926. (Women have been employed in the assorting room ever since the plant opened. Sixty were employed at that time, and the number was steadily increased. The work was light, consisting of turning over plates of tin cut to required size and examining them for defects.) About 1934, 145 employees owned stock in the United States Steel Corporation, 825 owned their homes, and 650 owned automobiles. A pension system was established; and, in 1934, there were 72 pensioners, 1058 members of the employees' insurance association, and 1270 members of The American Works Relief Association. The pensions were paid from the income of a fund created by Andrew Carnegie and the United States Steel Corporation. This was available to men who had reached the age of 65 and had worked for the company 25 years or more and to women of 55 who had worked 25 years or more. There are in Elwood former employees who have been receiving a pension of sixty dollars a month for ten years. In 1933, a joint employees' and business men's organization held a Tin Plate Appreciation Day.

Several influences, however, tended to end the career of the tin plate plant. The failure of gas was the first of these, although this plant was one of those which were not forced to close by that failure. A new process of treating the steel so that it could be cold-rolled was invented. The mills at Gary and some other points installed this method, but its introduction here would have required the scrapping of a large part of the machinery in the plant. This process is scientific; the hot mill process is personal. The former is absolutely accurate and is not dependent upon the characteristics of the operators; the latter is highly personal and requires trained judgment in order to determine proper temperature and treatment. Consequently, cheaper labor may be used in the new process. As a result, the mill has been unable to meet competition with mills equipped with the latest machinery and has been closed for about three years.

So ends the saga of the tin plate industry in Elwood. It has been treated here at considerable length because it has played such an important part in the history of Elwood. It caused thousands of people to make their homes here; it brought other industries here; it was responsible for innumerable indirect changes in the life of the city. That the city has survived the loss of this industry so successfully is a tribute to the solidity of the industrial structure of the city and of the energy and vision of the forces which have brought other industries to replace this mammoth one, which had expanded to cover 33 acres.

This extensive treatment is justified also by the consideration that the social and economic problems connected with it influenced the thinking of the real subject of this book—Wendell Willkie. Here in small compass have existed most of the economic problems of our time—and social ones, too. Unemployment, wasteful exploitation of natural resources, the disappearance of one of our chief natural resources, the presence of great industries as well as small, labor problems, the problems of the employers in a most acute form, the rise and disappearance of industries, and other problems of great importance were evident here without the glamour and without the distortion that they receive from distance or from association with other great problems in great centers of population. With the training in clear thinking given him by his father, with the opportunities to observe these conditions at first hand, Wendell Willkie could have had no better laboratory in which to study social and economic problems. His youthful associations were with the children of working people as well as with those of the professional group, and he seems never to have known that there were distinctions to be made because of the status of the parents. There never has been in Elwood a distinction between "classes", no one living "across the tracks", as in some communities. There have never been either extremely poor nor extremely rich in the community.

One of the interesting influences of the tin mills in Elwood was the organization of the First Baptist Church in 1890. It met with twenty charter members in the old Presbyterian meeting house, now the Wesleyan

Methodist church building, in January, 1890. The influence of the mills is shown by the fact that their first hymn books were printed half in English and half in Welsh, as the congregation was about evenly divided between Welsh and English-speaking members.

Glass Industry

Another industry brought here by the discovery of gas was the glass industry. Because of its geological history, the community was able to supply abundant quantities of sand suitable for glass-making; and the easily secured and regulated fuel made this an ideal location. In 1890, the Macbeth-Evans Glass Company erected its first building in Elwood. A special train brought 365 glass workers from Pittsburgh to Elwood to work in this plant. Glass-blowing was all done by manpower, and it could not be done by unskilled labor. Glass-blowers received as high as thirty to thirty-five dollars a day; so the influx of this number of highly paid workers was no unimportant event for the community. These workmen were free spenders, for, they said, "No machine can ever take our place." This belief was subsequently shattered, however; and, as in the tin plate mills, the number of workmen necessary for a given task was reduced; and wages declined.

At first the plant made only chimneys and lantern globes. It was, for a time, the only plant in the world which manufactured oil-tempered lamp chimneys. These chimneys did not crack when subjected to sudden changes of temperature and could even be dropped from the height of a table without breaking. Since oil was still the standard source of light throughout the world, it is no wonder then that these and other products of the Macbeth-Evans Glass Company *were* shipped to all parts of the world.

In 1891, the company made the first optical glass successfully produced in this country. Another company had been awarded the contract to produce lenses for the astronomical observatory in Tokio, Japan. Unable to overcome the difficulties, this company appealed to the Macbeth-Evans company, which produced the lenses to the entire satisfaction of the observatory.

With the failure of gas, however, the peculiar advantages of Elwood for this industry disappeared; and the plant closed down. It was dismantled in 1938.

Another important glass works located here was constructed by the Seiberling glass interests of Akron, Ohio. Building for these works began in 1889 and was completed in 1891. The works were known as the Diamond Plate Glass Company. At one time, it was the largest glass factory of its kind in the world. It was purchased by the Pittsburgh Plate Glass Company and renamed Works No. 7 of the Pittsburgh Plate Glass Company. It closed December 23, 1903, when the gas boom had collapsed.

The plant was allowed to degenerate; but, in 1914, the part of the plant still standing was repaired to make refractories for the Works No. 8, at Kokomo, Indiana. Glass is made by melting some form of silica, usually sand, with potash, soda, or some other alkali with a base such as lime. This requires tremendous heat, which necessitates the use of furnace linings which do not melt at the high temperatures used and which will not react chemically with the melting and molten constituents of the glass. Such linings are called refractories. Refractories have other uses, but those produced by the Works No. 7 are used chiefly in glass plants. In 1917, this works became the main manufacturing unit of the refractories department of the company and is still in operation.

Other Factories

In 1887, the year gas was discovered in the commons of Elwood, the Kokomo Manufacturing Company was founded in Kokomo by G. I. Sellers. At first, it made only materials for interior house work but later began the manufacture of kitchen cupboards. After the plant was destroyed by fire in December, 1904, the Elwood Business Men's Associaqion persauded Mr. Sellers to purchase and reopen the old Elwood Furniture Factory site in Elwood. On February 13, 1905, business operations were begun here under the name of the G. I. Sellers and Sons Company.

The plant now occupies one-quarter million feet of floor space and has over 300 employees. It manufactures a complete line of portable kitchen cabinets, utility closets, kitchen tables, and breakfast room furniture. Each year, the products of the firm are displayed at the various furniture marts throughout the country. The products of this company are sold throughout the world.

An industrial firm once of great importance in Elwood was the Indiana Box Company. Due to the great supply of timber in the region, it was able to produce boxes

Wendell Willkie at Eleven

Indiana University News Bureau.

The Home of Julia, Robert, Fred, and Wendell at Indiana University

very economically and its products were sold throughout the country. It and a large number of similar companies were combined into the Associated Box Corporation. It was one of the oldest industries in the city; but, due to the growing scarcity of lumber and the increasing use of cardboard boxes, it gradually declined. The plant was dismantled in 1938.

The Elwood Lawn Mower Company was established here in 1898. It is still in operation, manufacturing sixteen models of hand lawn mowers.

Forge Works

A number of industries which were once important but about which little can now be learned were formerly in Elwood. There was an old forge works at South E and 21st Streets which made the shaft for the Ferris wheel which was so prominent an amusement feature at the World Columbian Exposition at Chicago in 1893. The Akron Steam Forge Company, probably a different company from the preceding, manufactured forgings of all kinds. It made both iron and steel forgings for steamships, marine and stationary engines, and locomotives. It produced both rough and finished forgings.

Diversity of Industries

Other plants brought here by the industrial boom were the McCloy Glass Works, manufacturers of lamp chimneys, lantern globes, etc.; the Elwood Boiler & Engine Works; the Superior Radiator Company; The Elwood Window Glass Company; the Vivisen & Weiskolp Bottle Works, manufacturers of caps and bottling machinery; the Phil Hamm Boiler Works; The Heffner Planing Mill Company; the Elwood Iron Works, manufacturers of gas well supplies and steam and hot water radiators; the Excelsior Works; the Elwood Box Factory; and the Elwood Furniture Company. This list indicates the wide diversity of interests which centered in Elwood in addition to the major industries. Those mentioned here have all disappeared, chiefly as a result of the failure of the gas supply which had seemed so "illimitable."

Their departure made great changes in the population and the general life of the community. Elmer Cox, printer, recently celebrated his golden wedding anniversary. At that time, he tried to make a census of Elwood people who lived here when he was married and discovered that there were probably not fifty people living here now who lived here at that time. Death, of course, has taken many of them; but, as in most American communities, distant fields have, for one reason or another, looked greener and have beckoned large numbers of them away.

RECONSTRUCTION

The collapse of the industrial boom resulting from the discovery of gas was, naturally, a great blow to Elwood. However, much still remained which could be salvaged. There were a great number of buildings which could be converted to other uses; there were excellent transportation facilities, including excellent railroad sidings; there was, above all, a large supply of efficient and industrial manpower. Several large firms continued operation; so there was no complete industrial collapse.

After the first reaction, the city set to work to persuade new industries to replace the old. In 1930, the Monticello Manufacturing Company, established in Monticello in 1921, moved to Elwood. It manufactures retail store equipment and display fixtures of various unusual design and construction.

In 1935, The Continental Can Company opened its Elwood Plant. It spent $500,000 in constructing new buildings and in equipping it for up-to-date can production. The American Sheet and Tin Plate Company was still in operation, and the Can Company purchased a part of its requirements from it but was compelled to buy other sizes and thickness of tin elsewhere. The presence of a large number of canning factories here was one of the determining influences in locating the plant here.

This company makes vegetable and fruit cans, condensed milk cans, and cans of similar nature for other products. It makes all the standard sizes up to #10, or gallon cans, as they are loosely called. It makes lacquer cans, tin cans lined with lacquer so that the contents do not touch the tin, and ordinary tin cans. These cans are made primarily for use in Indiana, but large quantities are shipped to Ohio, Michigan, Wisconsin, Illinois, and Kentucky. A few are shipped elsewhere. About a thousand carloads (a carload is 90,000 #2 cans— the ordinary canned corn can) of tin cans are shipped from this plant yearly, about three carloads a day. In addition, many more than that number of truckloads of cans leave the plant annually.

71

The plant has an average employment of about 125 throughout the year, but at the two peak seasons—the time of the pea pack and the time of the tomato pack— there is a very large increase in the number of employees.

On February 7, the National Trailer Company of Huntington moved its plant to Elwood. Its open house was attended by over 700 visitors. This plant has good prospects, for the use of trailers promises to increase greatly.

This summer, Elwood became the home of the National Book Company, formerly affiliated with a printing firm in Fort Wayne, Indiana. This company so far has published a number of textbooks for use in the public schools.

The city quite naturally has an unusual number of good retail establishments of all kinds. Many of these have been in Elwood for a long time and have become landmarks. The customary service shops, such as dry cleaners, barbers, and shoe repair shops give the people of Elwood the service usually found only in cities of larger size. Amusements of various kinds may be had without going to larger cities. The residences of the city give the citizens pride in their community, for they are, with few exceptions, well kept and the grounds show the pride of their owners. All these things, how- ever, follow rather than control the development of a community.

Elwood has a number of smaller industries which go to make up the general prosperity of the city but which have no special interest from the historical view. The time of the city's industrial importance is far from

Indiana University Extension Debaters, 1916   *Indiana University News Bureau.*

Indianapolis Star.

Miss Mary Sleeth, Willkie's Farm Manager, Visiting a Willkie Farm

ended. There is an increasing tendency to decentralize mammoth industries in large cities and to extablish subsidiary factories in smaller cities. Elwood offers unusual attractions to such companies. The presence of a variety of industries is a much more desirable situation than the dominance of one or two huge ones upon whose success the community is dependent.

UTILITIES

As the city grew, the problem of an efficient water supply became insistent. The Elwood Water Company began operation May 7, 1892. This company changed owners several times, and there were frequent conflicts with the city over rates. The water is supplied by thirteen artesian wells yoked together and pumped through the mains by the Holly direct pressure system. The water works was taken over by the city on January 11, 1940.

Another utility which has grown with the city is the telephone utility. In 1892, The Farmer's Bank, the Citizens' Gas Company, James H. DeHority, Charles DeHority, and William A. DeHority were connected by telephone. In 1893, The Central Union Telephone Company established an exchange here with eighty subscribers, one of whom was Herman F. Willkie.

In 1895, a franchise was granted the Pana Telephone Company, which also established an exchange here. This was taken over by the Overshiner Telephone Company. Both the Overshiner and the Central Union Telephone were operated by magnetos, the subscriber ringing the exchange operator by turning a crank on the side of the telephone box.

About 1901, the Delaware and Madison County Telephone Company opened an exchange and introduced the telephone run by a simple battery, which signaled the operator automatically when the receiver was lifted from the hook. This company bought out the Overshiner Company. The Central Union Telephone Company soon adopted this system and, in 1913, bought out the Delaware and Madison County Company. The Indiana Bell Telephone Company has operated the local lines since 1920.

In 1897, there was only one long distance circuit. This was connected with the exchange at Alexandria, Indiana. It is possible for the telephone company today to take care of any conceivable amount of business. From Elwood, it is possible to telephone to almost anywhere in the world, even to steamships.

As the original telephone exchange was necessitated by the growth due to the gas boom, some of the recent increases in the telephone service are due to the expected needs when Mr. Willkie makes his acceptance speech here. Expansion of the existing system had already been planned, but this event speeded up the plans.

As the population increased, the need of intra-city transportation became great, since most of the increase was due to the influx of workmen for the factories. In early times, workers lived near the factories where they were employed; but this custom has been less common in America, because workmen have not been inclined to feel bound to work in one place if the opportunities seemed better elsewhere. This is one of the more obscure manifestations of the spirit of liberty and independence among the working people of this land. Besides, it was not always convenient nor desirable for the newcomers to live near the plants where they worked.

So, in 1893, the year after the opening of the American Tin Plate Company, the Elwood Electric Street Railway Company began the operation of street cars here. The street car line extended for five miles, passing through the principal business and residence streets and extending to the city limits from the northwest to the southeast corners of the city. This line gave most of the inhabitants easy access to the business part of the city and to the numerous large and small factories which had come here to enjoy the benefits of the abundant cheap fuel.

With the advent of the automobile, the need of such transportation steadily declined. With the failure of the gas supply, too, Elwood passed through a period of declining population, the present population being about four thousand less than its peak population, in 1899. Consequently, the line was discontinued; but the Union Traction Company's interurban cars gave cross-city transportation until 1931.

Elwood I.O.O.F. Drill Team

Among the memorable events with which Elwood has been connected, the achievements of Captain John Nelson (Nett) Nuzum can not be forgotten. In 1882, the Anderson Temple, No. 9, of the Independent Order of Odd Fellows organized a military branch. Captain Nuzum, a shoemaker by trade, had received military training in the University of West Virginia and served in the state militia and was greatly interested in military maneuvers; so it was natural that he should take an active part in the organization and activities of this branch of the Odd Fellows. When Canton Elwood, No. 33, Patriarch's Militant was organized in Elwood in 1889, Mr. Nuzum was elected captain, since he was well-known for his efficiency in that work as a result of his success with the military work of the Marion Canton the preceding year: and he retained this position for thirty-six years.

The next year, The Elwood canton entered his drill team in the national contest at Chicago in Class C, as this required eighteen men and three officers and this was all the men he could muster. The team made a record of 93 per cent and won first prize in its class. Captain Nuzum received a score of 97 per cent as a commander.

The following year, he entered his team in the national contest at St. Louis, this time in Class A, which required twenty-four men and three officers. This time, the team made a score of 94.6 percent and won first honors for itself and its captain. The competition in this contest, according to Captain Nuzum, was very close. The decisions in this and all the other contests entered by his team were made by graduates of West Point.

In 1893, the canton entered the contest at the World's Fair at Chicago, representing Indiana in competition with cantons representing seventeen other states. The team made a score of 95.7 percent, winning from its closest rival by only .3 percent. Captain Nuzum considers this the crowning event of his career as a military commander and credits his success to the loyal support of his team.

For the next few years, there were no contests; but the canton gave many exhibitions, including one at the Diamond Anniversary of Odd Fellowship at Indianapolis in 1894. During all the years that Captain Nuzum commanded these drill teams, the team was active in the regular work of the lodge.

In 1900, the team entered the world contest at Indianapolis, making a score of 97 percent, the highest ever made by this canton. The team was especially well balanced in every respect, and there was never any doubt as to the outcome of the contest. The closest contestant made a score of 94.1 percent. On its return to Elwood, the team was received with such a greeting as can be compared only to that which a state championship basketball team would receive.

The last contest entered by the team was at Des Moines, Iowa, and was won without difficulty. Captain Nuzum still captains the drill team of the local canton. He is also a member of the Knights of Pythias and is captain of its drill team, which also exhibits his skill in this field.

A large number of minor events, important to the community and to individuals and worthy of note in a more extended history of the city must be passed by. In the early 1890's a police force and a fire department were organized. The present city hall was erected in 1899.

LIBRARY
A number of other enterprises and interests have helped to make Elwood a desirable home community. In 1898, a committee was organized to investigate the

possibilities of a library. Mrs. Herman .F Willkie, mother of Wendell L. Willkie, was secretary of the organization to secure a charter for the library. The committee had raised a thousand dollars by January 10, 1899; and in April, it opened with 1150 volumes and twelve magazines. In June, the library was turned over to the city.

Andrew Carnegie and other donors contributed to enable the library to construct the present library building, which was dedicated in 1898. At present the library has a branch at Frankton, which has about a thousand volumes, the remainder of the 16,663 volumes being in the library at Elwood. Besides serving the branch library, it serves three townships and the city of Elwood. During the year 1939, it lent to 6,799 card-holders 93,447 books. In addition, it has a large collection of clippings, pamphlets, and magazines.

Miss Edith Wilk, who was librarian for four months in 1916, is now Mrs. Wendell Willkie.

HOSPITAL

A step of great importance to large numbers in Elwood and its environs was the opening of the Mercy Hospital. The funds for its construction were raised by popular subscription, and funds for its support are raised by a tag day each year. It is administered and conducted by the Catholic Church. The hospital was opened November 15, 1926. Work on a large annex costing $100,000 was started September 17, 1935; and the annex was occupied May 12, 1936. It is one of the most adequately equipped hospitals in the state. It has beds for 44 adults and bassinets for 15 children.

Dealing with physical needs from another angle is Callaway Park, a 40-acre playground in the northeast part of the city. The gift deed by which Henry C. Callaway turned this land over to the city says, "Having at heart the health and happiness of all the people of the city, especially the working classes," and then proceeds to grant the land to the city for park purposes. This park is a beautifully wooded tract with swimming pool, tennis courts, football field, baseball diamond, playground, horseshoe courts, picnic grounds, and a pavilion. It is here that Mr. Willkie will make his speech accepting the Republican nomination for the presidency.

Other opportunities for wholesome physical recreation are offered by the W.P.A. recreation room on the third floor of the city building. Here are ping-pong tables, a handball court, and various more quiet games. Boys play in the high school gymnasium during the summer.

It has been impossible to discover just what contribution Elwood and Pipe Creek Township have made to the national defense. However, it is known that John H. Wagner, of Elwood, enlisted in the Civil War as a private and was discharged as captain of the 17th Indiana Volunteer Infantry (Wilder's Brigade). George L. Shaw, of Elwood, was discharged as a first lieutenant of the 75th Indiana Volunteer Infantry. There was at one time a large G.A.R. Post here; but death has taken all the members. Captain Wagner, who died May 1, 1939, at the age of 97 years, was the last survivor. Following the instructions of the Grand Army of the Republic, the charter of the local post was given to the library to be hung on its walls. Eighteen from Elwood served in the Spanish-American War.

During the World War, Elwood contributed liberally to the various Liberty Loans. In the first drive, it pledged $125,000; in the second, $625,000; in the third, it doubled its quota, pledging $300,000; in the fourth, it gave $461,100, exceeding its quota by $76,100. In the fifth drive, the city contributed liberally; but the exact records in regard to it are unavailable. Between four and five hundred for whom Elwood served as post office address served in the World War, a number as officers in the various medical and in other corps.

ASSOCIATIONS

It has been said that, whenever three Americans are gathered together, they proceed to make an organization, choosing a president, a vice-president, and a secretary-treasurer. Elwood is typically American in its tendency to form organizations for social, service, fraternal, and patriotic purposes. Below is a list of organizations in Elwood, with the dates of their organization:

Quincy Lodge No. 230 of the Ancient and Free Order of Masons—June 12, 1857.
Odd Fellows Lodge—May, 1858.
Order of Eastern Star—May 4, 1887.
Pythian Sisters—1887.
Daughters of Rebekah Lodge—1887.
Elwood Women's Relief Corps—July 23, 1888.
Elwood Knights of Pythias Lodge—1889.
Canton No. 33 of I.O.O.F. Lodge—1889.
Women's Club—October, 1897.

Benevolent and Protective Order of Elks Lodge— April 13, 1897.

Elwood Camp of Sons of Veterans—August 15, 1899.

Knights of Columbus Council—May 17, 1903.

Ladies' Catholic Benevolent Body—October 22, 1903.

Royal Neighbors of America, Camp No. 3812— June 20, 1904.

Delta Theta Tau Sorority—February 9, 1905.

Dorcas Club—March 5, 1908.

Loyal Order of Moose Lodge—March 6, 1910.

Phi Delta Kappa—June, 1910.

Iris Club—January, 1914.

Stet Club—1914.

Elwood Department Club—January 1, 1915.

U and I Circle—April 16, 1915.

Auxiliary of Moose Chapter—May 2, 1917.

Adair Circle of Ladies of G.A.R.—February 19, 1919.

Louis Monroe Post No. 53, American Legion— September 5, 1919.

Auxiliary of Elwood Legion Post—April 7, 1920

Kiwanis Club—February 1, 1921.

Elwood Council No. 46, Daughters of America— March 26, 1925.

Business and Professional Women—1925.

Junior Order of United American Mechanics—1927.

Sigma Phi Gamma Sorority—May 4, 1930.

Veterans of Foreign Wars Post—March 20, 1932.

Ladies' Auxiliary of V.F.W. Post—1932.

Kappa Delta Phi Sorority—May 20, 1932.

Omega Phi Tau Sorority—January 15, 1933.

National Council of Catholic Women—February, 1934.

Squadron of the Sons of American Legion—March 9, 1934.

Catholic Youth Organization—May, 1935.

Elwood White Shrine Circle—November 5, 1935.

Elwood Lions Club—November, 1935.

Auxiliary of Elwood Eagles Lodge—May 21, 1937.

Beta Sigma Phi Sorority—August 17, 1937.

Unions, church groups, and groups more or less closely associated with the government all give outlets for civic interest and good fellowship. The Elwood Industrial Bureau has been active in encouraging the industrial growth and welfare of the city.

Noted People

A large number of people of more than local note have lived in Elwood. Senator Davis, of Pennsylvania, has been mentioned. The first person to separate helium from oil well gas in Texas—Pierre Haynes—was once an Elwood citizen. John C. Mellette, author of a number of widely read novels, was born here August 4, 1888. Wendell Willkie was born in Elwood and made it his home until 1919.

Heritage

Here, then, is the city of Elwood "with all its glories and imperfections on its head". As Stark Young said some years ago, "Some people go through experience like a spoon through soup—without getting any of the flavor," but this is not true of the alert-minded, and there is no question about the alertness of Wendell Willkie's mind. This was his chief characteristic during those Elwood years. One root of his character, then, goes deep into this community; certainly he is not easily explained without reference to it.

But another root goes deep into the past in what to many is a more obvious fashion—through his heritage from his ancestors. In an interview published in *The Day*, a Jewish daily, Wendell Willkie said that anti-Semitism was "a possible criminal movement" and that the growth of such a movement would be a calamity. He said that he had appealed for national tolerance and religious liberty long before he even thought of being a Presidential candidate. With his knowledge of history, he doubtless knew that nations which had driven out "undesirable" social groups had done so to their own sorrow. When the Spaniards drove the Jews and Moors out of Spain, they drove out their intellectual progress and their prosperity. The religious wars and persecutions in Flanders drove out, not only the Protestants, but the hat industry. The persecution of the Huguenots drove out of France the lace industry. Such things are material losses, but there are also spiritual and intellectual losses to a nation that persecutes or drives out groups of its citizens. Mr. Willkie insists that what is needed in the nation today is national unity, and that can never be attained through the separation of races or classes through hatreds and persecutions.

If he knew nothing but the history of his own family, Mr. Willkie would be aware of this same fact. On both sides of his family, his forefathers came to America to escape the harsh conditions of life in Germany which those who wished to think and speak and act with freedom had to face.   Mr. Wendell Willkie has said that, in all the history of his family, he and his five brothers and sisters have been the first to know from birth the blessings of freedom.

Maternal Line

On the maternal side, his ancestors were participants in that upsurge of European liberalism that marked the era culminating in 1830.   In November of 1829, Louis Ludwig Treusch, great-grandfather of Wendell Willkie, his wife and two children, his brother Adam and Adam's wife and six-month-old daughter, and unmarried brother George left Erbach, in the Odenwald, Hessen-Darm-stadt, Germany, and sailed from Le Havre, France, before the end of that year, arriving in Baltimore early in 1830.   George at once enlisted in the American army, where he served until 1849, having fought in Mexico during the war of 1848.

Louis Ludwig, his wife, his five-year-old daughter, and his one-year-old son Lewis settled at York, Penn-sylvania.   Five years later, the family moved to Bucyrus, Ohio, where Louis Ludwig conducted a blacksmith shop and manufactured wagons until 1853, when he bought a farm a few miles west of that city.   About the time of the Civil War, the family anglicized the name to Trisch, from which it easily became Trish.

Lewis Trish, the oldest son, moved to Indiana about 1852 and made his home in Warsaw.   His wife, Etta

Trish, was a temperance lecturer for the Women's Christian Temperance Union, traveling from city to city to lecture and occasionally preaching as well as lecturing. She was a Presbyterian. One daughter of this couple became a doctor and married a doctor. Her husband by a second marriage was an architect.

Another daughter was Henrietta Trish. She attended the Indiana State Normal School, now the Indiana State Teachers College, at Terre Haute, Indiana. She taught in the grade school at Milford, Indiana, where she became aquainted with the superintendent of schools, Herman F. Willkie, and married him at her home in Warsaw the summer that he left Milford to teach at Lagro.

WILLKIES COME TO ELWOOD

The latter was also of German descent. He was born in Aschersleben, Germany, in 1857, the son of Joseph William and Minna Mathilda (Breitschuh) Willcke. Joseph William had been a student in a German university during the second great liberal movement that swept over Europe in the first half of the Nineteenth Century. After that failed, in 1848, he found himself *unpopular* with the authorities. Dissatisfied with conditions under the autocratic monarchy, Joseph William came to America in 1858. The wife and three children— Herman F., William Frederick, and Theresa—followed him in 1861. The family made its home on a farm ten miles south of Fort Wayne, Indiana.

Herman's father was a Catholic, but his mother was a Prostestant. Brought up as a Catholic to the age of nine, he began to attend Protestant services with his mother. At about the age of twenty, he became a Methodist.

At home, he was taught by his parents to speak, read, and write German. The only school was two miles from his home, and the roads were impassable during a large part of the year. The school terms seldom exceeded four months a year. No school, however, is too poor to provide an opportunity for one who desires to learn; and Herman Willkie taught winters and attended summer schools, working between times.

Desiring to attend Valparaiso College, which at one time had a larger student enrollment than any other college or university in America, Herman worked on a farm and dug ditches to pay his way through a year there. Including tuition, board, books, and other expenses, the year's schooling cost him $113.50. The next summer, he worked in the harvest fields and that winter taught school in Allen County.

Then he entered Fort Wayne College, a Methodist school, and, alternating college and teaching, finally graduated in 1884. After graduation, he became superintendent of schools at Milford, Indiana. Here he first met Henrietta Trish, one of the teachers, and married her after he gave up his position there to teach at Lagro, Indiana. One of his pupils there tells that money was scarce and the new principal walked to Lagro from Claypool, twenty miles away.

Herman Francis Willkie (as he now spelled the name) and Henrietta P. (Trish) Willkie came to Elwood in 1888, where he had secured the position of superintendent of schools. The Elwood schools at that time were ungraded, and his first tasks were to grade the schools and to organize a high school. At that time, Elwood had a population of less than a thousand. Gas had just been discovered the year before, and the great expansion of Elwood was just beginning. Three years later, it became a city. As will be seen, the history of the Willkie family was closely associated with the city of Elwood from its very beginning.

At that time, it was not necessary to attend a law school in order to be admitted to the bar. All that was necessary was to read enough law to be able to answer the questions put him by the circuit judge and to have certifications as to his character from a number of people who knew him. It is true that the laws were much fewer and were simpler than many of those on the statute books today; but it must not be forgotten that great lawyers could be developed by such a course if they had a love for the law, the ability and inclination to read, and a keen mind. Webster, Clay, Calhoun, and Lincoln learned their law and learned to speak without the help of a law school. This is mentioned to preclude the idea that good lawyers *could* not be developed by that method. Of course, it must be remembered that all were on an equality in this respect in the earlier days and that many still living can remember when lawyers with specific training in their profession began to appear.

The first three years of Mr. Willkie's residence were full ones (a characteristic of all his years). He was organizing the schools, instituting a high school, doing the actual carpenter work on the house at 16th and North B Streets, where he lived until 1891, and it is difficult to know what else, for he was not a man to be idle. Nevertheless, he found time to read law; and he was admitted to the bar and began practice in 1891.

As the city grew—from about a thousand in 1888 to 2500 in 1891 to about 15,000 in 1899—the need for lawyers became greater. There were a considerable number of lawyers, but many of them stayed but a short time. The legal business connected with the partition and transfer of real estate and for the establishment of new businesses must also have greatly increased.

In 1891, also, Mr. Willkie purchased the property at the corner of South A and 19th Streets in Elwood and moved into the one-story house there in October of that year. The deed, however, was not recorded until December, 1891. The family lived in this house until June of 1894, although it was sold in October, 1893. It was in this house that Lewis Wendell Willkie was born on February 18, 1892. This has been much disputed; so it may be well to give the evidence. When Mr. Willkie bought the house, he was anxious to get moved on account of Mrs. Willkie's condition (Wendell was born February 18, 1892) and the tenant A. C. Yelverton, who worked in a cabinet factory, was greatly disturbed by the necessity of moving, as Mrs. Yelverton was in the same condition. At first, according to their daughter, who still lives in Elwood, he thought of moving out of the city; but his foreman was building a house and persauded him to move into it, which he did before the plaster was dry. In a letter from Julia, the oldest child of Herman Willkie (who lived in this house from her

Indianapolis Star.

Robert and Donald Berkemeir on a Willkie Farm With Their 4-H Club Calves

Lewellyn.

Wendell's Uncle Frank and His Wife

sixth almost to her ninth year), to the present occupants of the house, she definitely states that Wendell was born in the southeast room downstairs—the parlor—of this house. She describes the furniture and tells about the coming of the telephone and the tin plate mill during the time the family lived in this house. The same location is given by Wendell as the place of his birth; but this, of course, would be only his recollection of what other members of the family had told him. The original name of this street was Simmons Street and was changed during the Willkies' residence there.

The family next moved to the northeast corner of 23rd and North A street, where they lived until June, 1900, when they moved to 1836 North A Street. While the family lived at 23rd and North A Streets, Elwood was still frequently flooded; and it was almost impossible to have cellars or basements. Mr. Willkie, however, devised a special drainage system to a ditch west of the present Central school building and constructed a small storage cellar under the kitchen. The Willkie children did a profitable business selling to the children who came from far and near the right to lie on the ground by the cellar window and look into this curiosity.

THE WILLKIE CHILDREN

All of the children are still living, and the careers of all have been out the ordinary. Julia, the oldest child, received both her A.B. and A.M. degree from Indiana University. Before graduating, she taught school in Elwood. At one time while attending Indiana University, she and three brothers rented an apartment; and she did the housekeeping in addition to her school work. After graduation, she taught at Bloomington, Indiana. Then she taught foreign languages at North Manchester, Indiana. During the World War, after taking a special course in accountancy, she became associated with the War Trade Board, being an investigator of importing and exporting companies. Later, she was in charge of the correspondence unit in the negotiations for bringing back war dead from foreign graveyards. Upon the completion of this work, she went to Europe, visiting the original home of her father. She took a course in bacteriology at Massachusetts Institute of Technology. As all the children had left home, she returned to her parents at Elwood, and taught German and geometry in the high school there. (She had learned German at school, for the parents spoke only English in their home). Then she became her father's partner in the law firm of Willkie and Willkie. She did most of the office work, but occasionally represented the firm at court. She is now employed as bacteriologist and chemist at Clark's Winery, St. Catherines, Ontario.

Robert T. Willkie, the next child, was born October 9, 1887. He received his A.B. degree from Indiana University in 1909 and his LL.B. degree in 1911. He received the degree of LL.M. from George Washington University in 1912. He returned to Elwood and practiced law there, being deputy prosecuting attorney. The United States entered the World War in April, 1917; and Robert entered the first Army Officers' Training Camp at Fort Benjamin Harrison and was commissioned a second lieutenant. After the conclusion of the war, he received a regular commission and remained in the Quartermaster's Department until his resignation in 1937, at which time he held the commission of major. He was stationed at numerous posts—Washington, D. C.; Camp Taylor; Fort Benjamin Harrison; Chicago; Boston; and New York among others. Twice he was stationed in the Philippine Islands, once for two years and the second time, just before his resignation, for two and one-half years. He is now assistant vice-president and the productions manager of the Seagram Distillery at Louisville, Kentucky. His wife is the former Pearl Moore, of Elwood. Both Julia and Robert were born before their parents moved to Elwood. All the other children were born in this city.

Herman Fred, Jr., known by the family as Fred, was born September 31, 1890. He graduated in 1912 from Indiana University, where he specialized in chemistry. He completed his college work in December, 1911, and went to Porto Rico as chemist for the Fajardo Sugar Company and was unable to return for his commencement exercises. During the World War, he was employed by the American Celluloid Company in New Jersey, whose work was considered an essential war industry. Then he was engaged in research work for the United States Industrial Alcohol Company and for the Corby Company in Canada. In 1926, he was employed by Walker's Distilleries and built a plant for them in Peoria and in Scotland. He is now vice-president at Seagram's.

Almost five years after Wendell's birth, Edward, the youngest son was born, December 25, 1896. He attended Elwood high school a year and a half but completed his high school course at North Manchester, where his sister Julia was teaching. Then he attended Indiana University and Oberlin College, each for a part year. Then he received an appointment to the United States Naval Academy. He was on the football team for two years, being on Walter Camp's All-American football team for 1920-1921. He was a three-letter man at Annapolis for two years, being proficient in football, wrestling, track, and lacrosse. He held the intercollegiate wrestling championship and represented this country in the 1920 Olympics at Antwerp in the unlimited weight class. He won second place, being thrown by a Finn. During the war, he served as a naval officer. He graduated from the Naval Academy in 1921.

He resigned from the navy to become football coach at Marion Military Academy, Marion, Alabama, but left this to become associated with Libby, McNeil, and Libby, of which he is now vice-president. He erected a plant for this company at Louvain, Belgium, and was general manager for this company and Swifts, jointly, for Belgium, Luxemburg, Switzerland, and the Saar region.

The youngest member of the family, Charlotte, was born October 24, 1899. After graduating from Elwood High School in 1917, she attended Indiana University for part of a year. Then she went to Washington and served in the correspondence department of the Red Cross at Washington, D. C., during the war. She gave full time to this the first year; but, the next year, she worked only part time, attending the Colonial School for Girls in

Where Wendell Willkie Found More Than Books

She Believed in His Future

Washington part time. Visiting her brother at Annapolis, she met his roommate, Paul E. Pihl, of Swedish descent but a native of Illinois, and married him on the day of his graduation in 1920. Her husband was in the upper ten percent of the class and was sent for training in aviation construction to Massachusetts Institute of Technology. Since graduation, he served twenty years in the United States Navy and attained the rank of lieutenant commander. She and her husband now reside in Berlin, where he is an attache in the American embassy.

The Mother

For some years after the birth of Wendell, Mrs. Rauner, the mother-in-law of Frank Willkie, the brother of Herman Willkie, lived at the home of the latter; and later the Willkies kept a housekeeper for some time. This gave Mrs. Willkie some leisure, which she used to read law. On March 15, 1897, after the birth of Edward, she applied for admission to the bar. Her admission to the bar was strongly objected to by some of the able attorneys of the county, but she appeared in her own behalf and at once made her reputation as a lawyer. She was the first woman to be admitted to the bar in Madison County, and perhaps in Indiana. She assisted her husband in his law office, and at one time opposed and defeated him in a case at court.

In a recent letter concerning Wendell Willkie's parents, Senator James J. Davis, of Pennsylvania, formerly of Elwood, says: "I went to Willkie's office at times to borrow a book. The Willkie office seemed to be open always. They would open it early in the morning and it would stay open until late at night. It was a question in my mind if they closed at all if they were practicing in the surrounding county seats. Willkie was a good talker.

"The father belonged to several fraternal societies of which I was a member and he took an active part. He was very much interested in the public questions of that day. As I recall, he was a great friend of William Jennings Bryan. He might be called a liberal Democrat. Mrs. Willkie was a very bright woman, and also a very able pleader before the bar." This letter refers to the father and mother of Wendell Willkie.

Much has been said about the lack of meals in the Willkie home. The fact of the matter is that the Willkies had good substantial meals, but meals that required little preparation. Robert remembers that his mother baked all their bread until he was about ten or twelve years old. Mr. Willkie would lay in a plentiful supply of apples and potatoes and would sometimes buy a stalk of bananas. Mrs. Willkie liked to undertake big tasks that she could devote all her energy to, but she disliked the smaller tasks of the household. Consequently, the family often ate one-dish meals. There were always meat and potatoes. Between meals, the children might raid the apples or snatch a banana from the stalk as they went through the house.

Mrs. Willkie liked to can. The standard pack for a year was 200 quarts of fruit and about a hundred glasses of jelly. Sometimes, almost three hundred cans of fruit were put up. She did not can vegetables, however; very few housewives at that time knew how to can them successfully. Moreover the family cared very little for vegetables. When Mrs. Rauner prepared meals for the family, she was rather hurt that they would not eat the vegetables she prepared.

Mrs. Willkie was very energetic until she was about fifty-five years of age. She had a large house and six children, but she kept the house spotlessly clean. Occasionally, she hired a girl to help; but, of course, while engaged in the practice of law, she kept a housekeeper.

Besides, she had considerable artistic ability. She painted china well. Most of her artistry, however, was devoted to needlework, in which she had remarkable skill. She did drawn work and embroidery rivaling imported Chinese work. She liked to make clothes and did make a great many garments, cutting her own patterns. One who knew her well and has had many opportunities to see needlework says that many are able to do one kind of needlework unusually well but few, like Mrs. Willkie, excelled in all kinds.

Mrs. Willkie, like Herman Willkie and the children, was a voracious reader. There was no library near until 1899; so the Willkies had accumulated a library of between five thousand and six thousand books. From this, it is easy to see why the family was sometimes in financial straits. This library was not intended for display to impress visitors but was bought to be read. In the last years of her life, she was still a steady reader, reading two or three books a week. She liked all kinds of books and read many recent novels because she was familiar with most of the older ones. Among the last books she read were *Gone With the Wind* and *Grapes of Wrath*. Her very last book was the *Bounty Trilogy*.

Several years before the death of Mr. Willkie, he had left the house at 19th and North A Streets and established an apartment at 1449½ South A Street. Then he took a trip to Belgium, where Edward was stationed. When their house was given up, their large library was divided. About 1500 old, out-of-date books were sold to secondhand dealers, along with the furniture. Some of the law books were taken by Wendell, and others were sold to Indiana University. Those which the University did not care to buy were given to it. A good collection of books on the Bible were given to the Elwood Public Library. Some had been lost in the fire on Thanksgiving Day, 1910, a fire resulting from a defective fireplace, doing about $1500 damage to books, furniture, and other household articles, and compelling member of the family to live with friends until repairs could be made. The loss was covered by insurance. Besides, each of the children took a number of books. Robert and Wendell each have libraries of about 2500 volumes.

Mrs. Willkie's interest in reading went beyond her own home. Soon after her death, the following communication from the Elwood Public Library was published in the Elwood *Call-Leader* of March 13, 1940:

"The Elwood Public Library has lost a friend in the death of Mrs. H. F. Willkie. She was closely associated with the local library, being one of the founders. Mr. and Mrs. Willkie were members of a committee which met November 26, 1898 and which decided to solicit subscriptions at ten dollars a share for a $1,000 fund for a free public library. The first page of the first minute book of the Elwood Library Association has first the name of H. F. Willkie and then Henrietta Willkie. They were elected trustees of the library January 25, 1899, when the first fifteen directors were chosen to start the Elwood Library. Mrs. Willkie was elected the first permanent secretary of the library board on February 14, 1899. Mr. Willkie drafted the articles of incorporation for the library charter.

"But Mrs. Willkie's close association with the Elwood Public Library did not end then. In 1917 her son, Wendell, became a member of the Library Board. He married Miss Edith Wilk who had been the librarian during part of 1916.

"Mrs. Willkie's son, Robert, married Miss Pearl Moore, who had been assistant librarian at the local library before her marriage.

"Then Mrs. Willkie's niece, Julia, daughter of Frank Willkie, was the first assistant librarian at the Elwood Public Library from 1927 until her marriage to Edward Sturbois in 1937.

"After the death of Mr. Willkie, 26 of his books on religion and a framed map of Elwood for 1906 were given to the Elwood Public Library.

"Just last month Mrs. Willkie's son, Wendell, gave the book he had reviewed: "The Young Melbourne" to the local library.

"Mrs. Willkie continued her interest in the Elwood Public Library to the last, having been there less than a week before her sudden death.

After the death of Mr. Willkie, Mrs. Willkie preferred to live for a time at a private home in Maryland; but, about two years before her death, she returned to Elwood and made her home with her son Robert's sister-in-law, Mrs. Grover C. Montgomery, at 1402 South F Street. During this time, Mrs. Willkie was very active. She walked to the library almost daily, she walked to visit a crippled man with whom she liked to discuss questions, she crocheted garments for babies, and did many other things for the love of doing them. There she had a heart attack one Saturday evening and died the next day with little pain, March 10, 1940.

THE FATHER

The greatest influence in the lives of the children was that of their father. Concerning him, Robert says, "No one could be closer to boys than my father. No one could instil democracy better, but he never preached to us. He was an extraordinary man. He could understand the other fellow's side and took up their problems with them as if it were fun.

"We boys felt that we could never let Father down. We could not lie. If we got into mischief at school we admitted it to the teachers and to Father. He taught us that we must work; that we must get our lessons; that we must believe in the rights of man. He could understand anything from a bellyache to a marriage problem. Father was without a peer."

He took more interest in children than ordinary fathers did. He wanted his children to have an education.

He often told them that fortunes could be taken away from them but that they would always have their education. He was gentle in talking with children and had their confidence.

He helped the boys with their lessons. He woke them in the mornings with quotations from literature, and he used to read them a chapter in some book every night. He never whipped nor scolded them, but they felt that they could not betray his trust in them. The boys all went to work early, not chiefly because they needed the money, but because he taught them that it was right to work. His greatest happiness was in what his boys were doing. Upon his tombstone is carved truthfully, *"He dedicated his life to his children."*

Herman Willkie was considered by his community as a better than ordinary trial lawyer. He was a real crusader. He could have had retainers from the various corporations in and about Elwood, and these would have given him a steady income. He preferred, however, to represent those who could not afford retainers and who had no reason to give them. Consequently, his income was uncertain. Some years, it might be very high; other years very low.

He never represented the corporations, but he often represented the unions. Unlike practically all other lawyers of his time, he would never accept a railroad pass. At that time, there were no employees' compensation laws; and he frequently represented injured employees. Like all the other lawyers in towns of such size, however, his practice was general, for there was little opportunity for specialization.

At the entrance of this country into the World War, he might have made money; but he preferred to travel about among the German-speaking people in this and surrounding areas and urge them to give their full support to the United States. He was very successful in this, but it caused him to greatly neglect his practice.

Soon after he arrived in Elwood, he began to buy up real estate and did accumulate a moderately-sized fortune in that line, erecting altogether over two hundred houses, which he sold to workmen who came to the city. When the gas failed, however, the value of these investments was greatly depreciated. Professor Paul Harmon, of Indiana University, a close friend of Wendell Willkie in their school days in Elwood and at Indiana University, says that Mr. Willkie was able to largely finance his children's way through college as a result of the sale of a row of houses along the railroad. At one time, Mr. Willkie was owner of a canning factory. However, he was not a good business man; and his fortunes were continually up and down.

He was intensely interested in Elwood. A workman who knew him said recently, "Mr. Willkie thought there was no place like Elwood. He was for Elwood tooth and toenail." He was interested in the schools, in the churches, and in the general welfare of the community.

There was considerable violation of the law by the saloons, but it was difficult to get convictions. One night, the chief of police arrested a saloonkeeper who had been arrested frequently before but had always gone free. The city attorney expressed the wish that he had Mr. Willkie to help him in the case; so the chief, who

The Willkie Brothers Visit During Convention

Wide World Photo.

Anderson Street, Elwood Indiana
Upstairs at Extreme Right, Wendell Willkie Practiced Law

did not personally know him, asked him to help the city attorney. He did, and the man was convicted. A few days later, the chief met Mr. Willkie and offered to pay him, since he had called him on the case. Mr. Willkie positively refused to take any payment. A short time afterwards, the chief of police learned that the saloon-keeper had offered Mr. Willkie $200 to defend him in this case.

On January 2, 1922, Herman Willkie became city attorney and served two terms. One of the problems before the city at that time was the proposed increase of rates for water service. Mr. Willkie insisted that, if the water company would extend its lines, as large number of people wished it to do, and secured more customers, the company would make more profit than it would by limiting its service. This is of interest in connection with the comparable policy undertaken by his son, Wendell Willkie, in his management of the Commonwealth & Southern Utilities.

Both Mr. and Mrs. Willkie were profoundly religious. Both came from homes of divided religious views and so had come to have a tolerance for others' views. Mr. Willkie had originally been brought up in the Catholic faith but had become a Methodist. Mrs. Willkie was a Presbyterian; but, after her marriage, had joined the Methodist Church. Soon after his arrival in Elwood, Mr. Willkie began to teach an adult Sunday School class and continued this for many years; and Mrs. Willkie taught a children's class. He collected a valuable library on the Bible and studied it. As a result, he was able to present the lessons in such a way as to build up the largest Sunday School class in the city. Besides this, he served as Sunday School superintendent and as a steward and trustee of the church. The children were baptized and the older children were received into full membership in the Methodist Church.

After some years, however, they left this church. There was a mortgage on the church property, and the holder of the mortgage had not been able to secure payment nor satisfactory assurances in regard to it. So he employed Mr. Willkie to bring suit. Believing that the mortgagor should receive satisfaction, he took up the matter with the church, but without effect; so he filed suit. This brought the desired activity. The church aroused itself and paid off the mortgage. However, so much ill feeling had been aroused that the Willkies decided to transfer their membership to the Presbyterian Church. Julia, who had been teaching Sunday School there, also transferred hers; but Wendell had already transferred his to the Episcopal Church. An old neighbor says that Mr. and Mrs. Herman Willkie never missed a Sunday going to church, walking arm in arm down the then unpaved street.

Mr. Willkie died November 27, 1930, and was buried November 30 in the Elwood Cemetery. He still lives in the memories of his old friends and even in the hearts of many who never knew him personally as one who loved mankind and the welfare of mankind.

Elwood Days

This, then, was the sort of family into which Wendell Willkie was born on February 18, 1892. It is true that a man can overcome the handicaps of his early years and that he may drift away from their influences. Possibly this is easy in a family without deep-seated interests, in which family ties are weak, or in which the family tone is neutral. The Willkie family, however, was far otherwise. Each member was an individual, and his individuality was encouraged. There was no attempt to secure conformity. Each member was fully given the liberty that each desired for himself. It was, in effect, a democracy with equal rights for all, so far as this condition could be secured. Therefore, the members were opinionated and vocal in their opinions. This undoubtedly seemed strange to those who valued conformity and acquiescence. Certainly, each child born into this family had thrust upon him the responsibility of thinking for himself and of defending his thoughts. Education began, then, at a very early age.

There were four Willkie boys; and, to large numbers of Elwood people, they were indistinguishable. As recollections are examined and brains cudgeled to recall events of thirty, forty, and almost fifty years ago, no wonder if the sins and virtues of all the Willkie boys, and perhaps of the girls, are unloaded upon the head of one. So the stories of Wendell's Elwood days must be approached cautiously. One thing must constantly be borne in mind—the tales of those youthful days are not tales of loneliness. Universally, Wendell is credited with being one of the crowd. Therefore, what he did was largely in harmony with the common customs of the time and were done in company with the other children of his age. That he was an active, red-blooded youth, there is no gainsaying; that he was vicious, or mean, or destructive, there is no evidence.

Probably everyone who has reached the half-century mark can recall pranks which would no longer be tolerated but which were then considered natural. In some of our soberest colleges, even the serious students were not above hoisting cows to the top of four-story buildings or bedding them in the parlors of the college dormitories. When we are told that Wendell Willkie followed their example and put a cow in the high school building, we must remember that this prank was not altogether original and that it was not done alone. The group of boys with whom he associated have now grown up into good substantial citizens, whose sons and daughters take part in the modern substitutes for their parents' pranks. This is not an attempt to whitewash anyone; but it is always a prime mistake to picture events out of their setting.

There were in Elwood at that time, as at all times and everywhere, vicious boys, boys who took delight in destruction for destruction's sake, in disorder for the sake of disorder. There is no record that such were in the group with which Wendell Willkie was associated.

One of the near neighbors of the Willkies for many years was Elmer Cox, printer. His son was one of the group with which Wendell was most closely associated, and Mr. Cox tried to make his back yard attractive to the boys as a playground. He erected a tent there, and the boys made that their headquarters. They played the usual boys' games—marbles, go-sheepy-go, drake and duck, etc.—there. Consequently, he and the boys be-

Hampshires on a Willkie Farm

Cherry Time on a Willkie Farm

came great friends. Another friend of the boys was "Doc" Hinshaw, the druggist, where the boys liked to loaf and talk. When Wendell returns to Elwood, he never fails to have a visit with these old friends.

The boys used to play under the street lights. Elwood had a curfew whistle then; and, when it blew, Wendell's mother—and the mothers of the other boys—expected them to come home. Boys who were out after the curfew were supposed to be out making trouble for someone.

There was a swimming hole somewhere on Duck Creek where the city park now is. The girls were forbidden to patronize it, to their regret; but all the Willkie boys did. Another test of manly powers was to walk to Mudsock (Dundee, now) and back. This test left the boys exhausted but (the next day) triumphant.

On January 27, 1901, shortly before his ninth birthday, Wendell was received into preparatory membership in the First Methodist Church of Elwood and was later received into full membership. He continued in this church until he was in high school, when he left the Methodist Church and became an Episcopalian. The Episcopalian congregation at that time consisted of about a dozen families who had been united into a mission from Anderson. Wendell was a lay reader in this congregation. He is still an Episcopalian, as are his son and wife. He had arrived at a stage of seriousness much earlier than his brothers and his friends, and they found it difficult to understand him. During his last year in high school, there was no one whose duty it was to mow the yard about the Episcopal Church. Much to the amusement of the other boys and amidst their vociferous teasing, he mowed the yard voluntarily, quite unmoved by their hilarity.

Another evidence of this seriousness was his habit of going to his father's law office, taking down a law book, cocking his feet on the desk as he had seen his father do, and reading. Some of the other boys found it hard to believe that anyone would read a law book of his own free will, let alone enjoy it, as Wendell seemed to do.

He and Paul Harmon were always close friends and took a great deal of teasing from each other; but, when Paul said one day in class that *lawyer* and *liar* were synonyms, Wendell failed to see the joke. He bristled up at once and gave Paul—and the rest of the class—a long lecture on the dignity of the legal profession.

But these serious moments alternated with times of hilarity, when he entered into the fun of his crowd whole-heartedly. In fact, whatever he did, he seemed to do with all his heart, and mind, and body. One night, his gang decided to give the skeleton which was used in demonstrations in the physiology class an airing. They entered the building through an unfastened window and secured the skeleton, which had already lost an arm and leg. Just as they were fastening the skeleton in a tree, a policeman came along. The boys fled to the home of the editor of the Elwood paper and told him of their plight. He promised to protect them if they would give their word that they would never do such a thing again. Of course, there would be no fun in repeating the performance; so they readily promised.

It was the tradition of the high school that the class numerals should be painted in some prominent place, another echo of college pranks. Class numerals were on fences, smokestacks, and other places that had appealed to the imaginations of previous classes. Wendell's gang decided that the front walk and stone steps leading to the school would be the most fitting place for them to make their mark. Such a work of art was not intended to be unseen, nor was it. When questioned, all the members of the class admitted their guilt. The principal's next problem was to find the part each boy had played in perpetrating the "crime." Each boy was put "on the spot" to rub off his part with the aid of a brick.

One day, however, he designed an amusement for the school solo. He came to school with one pants leg rolled up to the knee and one not so high. One stocking was green and one red. When he entered the schoolroom, he took off his coat and displayed his shirt sleeves held up by a pair of women's garters of different colors. Naturally, he received the reward of laughter from his schoolmates and a less pleasant greeting from the principal, who gave him a severe scolding and had him reduce his garb to a more decent condition.

School

Wendell started to school in the eight-room red brick building on the lot where the present junior high school and senior high school stand. Except for the period during which the school was conducted in various buildings while the present structures were being erected, all his grade and high school work was taken on this lot.

The first year of Wendell's high school course was not one to look back to with pride, as is evidenced by the copy of his high school scholastic record on page 119, which also shows what he could do when he tried.

The teacher who made the strongest impression upon him was Philip Carleton Bing, his English teacher. "Professor" (as the students called him) Bing was intensely interested in his subject; and, unlike most other teachers, permitted and even encouraged the students to express their opinions freely on topics which came up in class, even if the discussions did drift away from the topic occasionally. He also taught the junior class in public speaking, which was primarily a class in argumentation.

The large library of his parents and their wide interests had made the meetings of the family at mealtime and other occasions periods of lively discussion. They had views—decided ones—and they had no inhibitions about expressing them. With eight members of the family trying to make themselves heard, there was no lack of spirit. Argument was the very breath of Wendell's being, and the opportunities of indulging in it under the direction of Mr. Bing added zest to the whole high school course.

For several years, the other boys had been somewhat annoyed—to put it mildly—with his argumentation, for they were his continual victims. They felt that he argued with them primarily to show his superiority rather than from any convictions. About his sophomore year in high school, however, they began to feel that he

Elwood High School.

Record Of .... Wilkie Wendell .... Entered 1-29-06

Course of Study.	Latin				German				Mathematics				Science				History				English				
	Beginning Latin	Caesar	Cicero	Virgil					Algebra	Algebra and Geom.	Plane Geom.	Solid Geom.	Botany	Zoology	Physics		Ancient	Mediæval & Mod'n.	United States	American Literature and Comp. X X	X	X	X
Year	1	2	3	4	1	2	3	4	1	2	3	4	1	2	3	4	1	2	3	4	1	2	3	4
1st Term	P	P	E	G					G	G	E			P		E		E	E	G	G	G	G	
2nd Term	P	G	G						P	E	E	P		G	E			E	E	E	E	E	E	

Plan of Marking:—E, excellent; G, good; P, passed; C, conditioned; F, failed.
X— Composition three times a week. X Compositiod once a week.

	Physical Training	Music	Writing
No. of Credits		¼ ¼ ¼ ¼ / ¼ ¼ ¼ ¼	¼/¼

Graduated .... Jan. 28, '10.

.... M. C. Gerichs. ....

119

had grown up, matured, ahead of them and began to feel a deeper respect for him.

The class in argumentation discussed questions of national interest. It was the custom to secure three of Elwood's business men to judge the debates. One of the questions was "Resolved: That imigration be restricted in the United States." The affirmative captain was Katherine Henze and the other members of the team were Eunice Carter and Earl Whiteman. The negative captain was Wendell Willkie and two other boys. Miss Henze says that the boys were cocky. They felt sure that the girls would not be able to work up any arguments to meet them. The affirmative team, however, was determined to show the negative up. They worked hard and planned the debate with real teamwork, while the other team relied upon their natural ability to meet their arguments. The result was that the affirmative won. Wendell was bewildered, but he did manage to congratulate the winners. This was the only time, the girls say, that he was defeated in high school debate.

This love of debate remains as one of Mr. Willkie's characteristics. He cares less for formal argument than for the spontaneous kind that springs up in the course of conversation. Then he enters into it with his whole body and mind. He gets to his feet and gesticulates violently, for he dearly loves a wordy combat. In the last few years, he has enjoyed a Town Hall radio debate with Robert Jackson, United States Attorney General. *Fortune Magazine* is responsible for the statement that a high official in the administration consented to appear on a public program only after being promised that Mr. Willkie should not be his opponent.

One of his opponents in this school debate relates two other incidents of their school days. One day, Mr. Bing asked Wendell to recite the famous seven-ages speech from *As You Like It*. Wendell arose full of confidence and began in his most oratorical manner to recite, "All the world's a stage and All the men and women merely players." After a few lines, he was interrupted by a scream of laughter from the class; and the instructor laid his head upon the desk, shaking with laughter at Wendell's version of the passage. Wendell blushed like a school girl and sat down chagrined at his failure.

His confidence in attempting the quotation was justified by his familiarity with Shakespeare. It was not uncommon when the Willkie children were among a gathering at the home of some friend for someone to suggest that the Willkies present a play. These plays were spontaneous and unrehearsed. They would assign each other or assume parts and give the lines as nearly as they could remember them. If they could not remember the lines, they knew the story of the play and made up words to suit. The report is that *Hamlet* and *Macbeth* were a part of their repertoire.

On another occasion, the geometry class was assigned a very difficult problem in geometry. In the morning, everyone but Wendell was worried, for no one else had solved it. When the narrator of the incident asked him how to work the problem, he refused to tell her. So she determined that she would show him that a girl could get it too. When the teacher asked who had worked the problem, she raised her hand, too. Wendell looked daggers at her, especially when it was she who had the honor of putting the demonstration on the board. After class, he congratulated her on the solution.

He did not take a great interest in girls; but, about this time, he began to haunt the library and spent less time with the other boys. One of the high school girls was also very studious, and a strong attachment grew up between them as a result of their common interests.

Among the boys, Wendell cared little for appearance. Their entertainment was likely to be rough, and careful grooming was likely to be dissipated in a moment's frolic. At other times, however, as can be seen from the numerous pictures of him, he was very careful about his appearance. He may have worn untidy clothes in a time of revolt against the fastidious fraternity group at college; but, as a rule, he was more than ordinarily neat.

This was a period in which fraternities flourished in high schools and became such a menace and nuisance to the authorities that they were finally outlawed by the state legislature. The fraternity group in the Elwood High School were strongly inclined to snobbishness, something which was repugnant to the Willkie spirit. He was for a time a member of Beta Phi Sigma, but left it when the members put on airs with his friends. So he organized the mysterious club, the K. O. B. which parodied the snobbishness of the fraternity. Ultimately, it was discovered that the mysterious letters stood for *King of the Beasts*. This conflict with the fraternity influenced his career at Indiana University.

122

Wendell did not mature physically as early as his brothers did, and the family felt some concern about him. During the summer between his first and second semesters in high school, which he had entered at mid-year, he attended Culver Military Academy. He had begun to exhibit a slight stoop, and his father thought that the summer school at Culver might straighten him up. He could swim dog-fashion, but here he learned to coordinate his muscles so that the could swim with some ease and grace.

There was much hazing from the boys who had been at camp before, but Wendell was not the boy to be easily cowed. The result was that he and his roommate, also from Elwood, suffered more than most of the newcomers. However, he maintained his independence and finally won a degree of respect from the second-year boys. One of the hazers was from a very wealthy family but borrowed five dollars from Wendell and refused to repay it. At last, one of the officers learned of the affair, paid Wendell, and charged it up to the debtor's account.

The days were spent in drilling, swimming, rowing, and studying. Wendell learned to erect the masts and put up the sails and had some practice in sailing.

However, Wendell did not attain his full height of six feet two till he was about seventeen, whereas the older boys had reached this stage when they were fifteen. He did not begin to take on the Willkie weight (he now weighs about 210) until he was about twenty-four. He first made the Elwood High School football team in 1907, playing on the same squad with his brother Fred.

He did not play much throughout his high-school period and took little interest in athletics in college.

One of the great events of the high school was the banquet given by the junior class for the seniors. Thirteen juniors, nine of whom graduated the next year from Elwood High School, entertained the seniors in May, 1909. Wendell Willkie was toastmaster on this occasion. Besides the juniors and seniors, the banquet was attended by the superintendent, the principal, and the high school teachers.

One of the principles early ingrained into the young Willkies by their parents was that it was not honorable not to work. Whether there was need for money or not, the children felt that they should have some occupation. Wendell Willkie's first job was taking a cow from its stable near the center of Elwood to its pasture on the edge of town in the morning and back again in the evening. The time of his other employments is less certain, but he was never among the unemployed.

His brother Bob had made arrangements with a Cleveland advertising agency to distribute samples and other advertising matter from door to door. In time, Fred and Wendell took over this business. They received two dollars a thousand for delivering matter to the front door of every house in Elwood and three dollars a thousand when delivery was made to the back door. In their moments of idleness, the two amused themselves by describing the front and back doors of any house one might mention to the other.

A local wholesale house bought up potatoes in anticipation of a rise in price. When his expectations were disappointed and the potatoes began to spoil, he hired Wendell to sort out the good potatoes from the bad ones. He performed this distasteful task so energetically, that his employer is said to have prophesied that some day he would be president. Later, he sold bananas for the wholesale house.

Another salvaging task was separating nails from trash. The trash was made up of sweepings from factories, and a large horseshoe magnet was used to separate the nails from the rubbish. Wendell got a nickel a keg for picking out the nails and putting them in the kegs. At a nickel a keg, he could earn ten cents a day at this task.

The summer of 1907 was a hard summer for the farmers. Money was scarce but they had plenty of poultry and eggs. Starting out at four o'clock in the morning, Wendell drove a bakery wagon along the roads to Aroma and Perkinsville, stopping at farmhouses and exchanging bakery goods for poultry products.

After the failure of natural gas, many houses were moved from Elwood into the country. Wendell assisted in rolling these houses out of Elwood to be used as barns and storage houses.

Sometimes he worked in a department store. Some mornings, he began at six-thirty and worked to eleven or twelve o'clock at night for seventy-five cents a day. One of his fellow-workers says that he remembers that Wendell would always give good measure. When he filled an order for crackers, he would sometimes put in two or three extra ones with the remark that "they" might need them.

Wendell graduated from Elwood High School in January, 1910, and entered Indiana University for the spring term. Consequently, there was no break between high school and college life, as there is for so many. Besides, Julia, Robert, and Fred had preceded him to the campus; and the four lived together in a house rented from one of the professors. Here, Julia mothered the three brothers while completing her own college course. So Wendell entered at once into college life without the consciousness of a break in his existence. The Willkie home was the site of frequent gatherings of student friends, at which the Willkie hospitality was displayed without stint. At Elwood, Robert had learned to bake pies, at one time baking (with his brothers' assistance) forty pies for the Salvation Army. Naturally, he was called on to give evidence of his skill for his guests. Under the name of Fred Willkie in the 1912 *Arbutus* is the notation: "The Willkie brothers are better known than the Cherry sisters."

With four Willkies, trained through childhood in the art of holding their own in argumentation, at one table, their friend Paul Harmon says, eating was a minor affair to be indulged in when there was nothing left of the question they had been discussing. They lived on the keen edge of intellectual excitement. Wendell Willkie's academic career is briefly told. He entered the University in the winter of 1910 and attended summer school so that he could enter in the fall as a regular sophomore. He graduated with the class of 1913. His college record shows that he made 72⅔ hours of A, 74⅔ hours of B, and 10⅓ hours of C grades. He received his bachelor's degree in 1913, won the junior law prize in 1915, and graduated from the law school in 1916. It was not the custom to have a separate commencement for the law school; but, in 1916, it was planned to do so. Wendell Willkie was elected senior class orator for the class of eighteen legal aspirants.

In 1913, Woodrow Wilson had published *The New Freedom*. Willkie had been an ardent Wilson man in the 1912 campaign and had doubtless read the book. When he came to choose the subject for his senior law class oration, he chose this title for his speech. When Wendell walked out on the platform to present his oration, he was surrounded by the full bench of the Indiana Supreme Court and the entire faculty of the law school. It is easy to imagine their consternation when the young orator launched into a strong criticism of the law school and of its methods. Everyone was shocked. When the diplomas were distributed, he did not receive his. For two days, he was uncertain of his fate. At last, he was called to the offices of the university and given a strong private lecture—and his diploma! He was now a bachelor of laws.

But the academic side of college is far from being the whole of university life. This is the heart of college life to the earnest student; it is but the excuse for college life to many. There accompanies all this a full, vigorous, active life permeating the academic life, invigorating it, spicing it. As one of his brothers said recently, "If there was a shirt tail parade, Wendell was in it," which is to say that the college for the time was his whole existence. If anything was going on, he was in it. And there was always something going on.

When he entered the university, he found that the fraternities were ruling student affairs. There was a large group of non-fraternity students, some of considerable ability, who had little to say in student groups and activities. This was due to several causes: Many of the "barbs" (short for barbarians, since they were not "Greeks", belonging to Greek letter fraternities) were handicapped by lack of money for the extras which it was so easy for the wealthy fraternity members to secure. They dressed poorly, lived in the less desirable rooming houses, and boarded at economical boarding houses and earned their meals at a local restaurant. They worked at all sorts of odd jobs to eke out their slender funds and so had little time for the extra-curricular activities which took up so much of the time of the fraternity students. Since each fraternity tried to win to its ranks any student who showed more than usual ability either in scholarship or other activities, a disproportionate number of non-fraternity students were below the average in achievement of any kind. Besides, there was a large sprinkling of non-fraternity students who would have given their souls to be invited into a fraternity—or sorority; and these, naturally, could never be brought to organize against the fraternities.

Under his father's influence—and probably by nature, as well—Wendell had sympathy for the under dog. His experience with high-school fraternities had embittered him against these organizations; so, upon his arrival at the university, he threw himself wholeheartedly in the political fight between the "barbs" and the "frats". Some of his boyhood friends were in fraternities, and he continued his friendship with them. Through them, too, he made the acquaintance of fraternity members; but he could not help noticing the snobbish element in the fraternities, and he felt that they represented the fundamental spirit of these college organizations. Willkie, of course, was just "a country boy" and was, at first, completely ignored by the fraternities. But not for long.

He cared nothing for political office for himself, but he did care about breaking up the political monopoly held by the fraternities. When Paul Harmon, a schoolmate from Elwood, came to the university in the fall after Wendell entered, the latter set about to push him into the political arena. He managed the campaign and succeeded in having Harmon elected president of the sophomore class. This did much to break the power of the fraternities.

Prominent among the fraternities was the Beta Theta Pi, and prominent in this fraternity were Paul V. McNutt and Sherman Minton, now Federal Security Administrator and Senator from Indiana, respectively. To Wendell Willkie, they represented everything that he was opposed to; and they roused his fighting spirit. He fought and helped to win greater representation of non-fraternity students on the Indiana University Union Board. McNutt was an influential member of the Jackson (Democrat) Club, and Willkie determined to fight his influence and become one of its leaders. In the end, he became a member of the board of this club.

With the competition of the non-fraternity students, it became evident that a new political alignment was necessary on the campus. Consequently, the non-fraternity group and the Beta Theta Pi became political affiliates and together were able to dominate campus politics. When McNutt was fighting to become president of the Student Union, it was the co-operation of Willkie, who swung the non-fraternity vote, and of George W. Henley, a force in the Republican organization on the campus, that made his campaign successful.

All this non-fraternity activity came to a queer crisis. According to his roommate, Maurice Louis Bluhm, the latter came to their quarters one evening and found Wendell pacing the floor. It was some time before he could learn the cause; Wendell had been invited to join the Beta Theta Pi.

"Why don't you?" Bluhm asked.

"Well," replied Wendell, "if I don't, I'll lose my girl; and, if I do I'll lose my soul."

He discussed the matter with a number of other non-fraternity students and at last became a member of the Beta Theta Pi.

Sometimes the campus politics is very serious; sometimes it is merely a game. It is interesting as a contest between rivals and rival groups. In his senior year, at the class election, Wendell placed the name of a friend in nomination for treasurer of the class, although it was obvious that there was no chance for his election. The nominee asked to have his name withdrawn, but Wendell stood fast and would not accept the withdrawal. That winter, a new plan for college elections was presented

Typical Willkie Farm Scene

Indianapolis S'ar.

International News Photo.

Wendell Willkie, Mrs. Carrie Chapman Catt, and James E. West Receiving Awards for "Distinguished Service to Humanity" from National American Woman Suffrage Association

to the Student Union. There was a vigorous discussion, in which Willkie took active part, greatly, *The Indiana Student* reports, neglecting Robert's *Rules of Order*.

While in the college he became a disciple of Bob La Follette, the elder. La Follette was then crusading against the aggressions of big business. Willkie still calls himself a La Follette liberal, a point which will be discussed later in connection with his fight against the TVA. He became greatly interested in Adam Smith's *Wealth of Nations* and Karl Marx' *Das Capital*. With an inveterate love of argumentation, he helped to organize the Socialist Club, where topics of all kinds could be argued without gloves and where all kinds of views could be aired. He helped win for Indiana University a debate with De-Pauw University in his senior year, taking the negative of the proposition that the state should pass a compulsory insurance law especially adapted for wage-earners. He attended a meeting of the city council of Bloomington to insist that students should be permitted to vote in the city elections, as otherwise they would lose their vote or be compelled to return home for elections, which was an impossibility for most of them. The city council evidently looked upon this as a piece of student impertinence and ignored the request.

He was elected president of the Booster Club in December, 1912, for the winter term. Consequently, upon him fell much of the responsibility for the conduct of the third state basketball tournament, which had been initiated at Indiana University in 1911. In previous years, play in the tournament had been limited to winners of elimination contests; but, in 1913, competition was

133

opened to all schools belonging to the Indiana High School Athletic Association. Consequently, ninety-five schools competed.

In his senior year, also, Willkie was made a marshall. There had been considerable disturbances at athletic contests, and especially at football games. After some discussion between the faculty and students, it was decided to create a body of marshalls. These were to be "representative students, popular among the student body, possessing influential ability, and whose scholarship is above question." Lists of students considered suitable for this office were presented by some of the leading student organizations of the university, and a number of marshalls were chosen by the faculty from these lists. The duty of these marshalls was to police the stadium during athletic contests, to act as ushers at university functions, and to perform such other offices as might seem suitable.

But all was not serious with Willkie during these years. One of the favorite sports of the non-fraternity group of which he was a leader was to attend one of the local theaters and sit in the "pigeon roost", or balcony. Here they made themselves somewhat—or more—of a nuisance by their loud talk (This was before the day of the talking pictures), and so a guard was stationed in the gallery to see that matters were not carried too far. One night, the guard decided that the time for action had come. He seized an offending student, struck him over the head, and hurried him down the steps to a policeman. After the first shock of surprise had passed, the other students in the balcony rushed to

134

their comrade's defense, the three Willkie boys among them. A free-for-all fight ensued, the student was rescued, and all returned to see the conclusion of the picture. When Robert and Wendell reached home and took off their shirts, they discovered that someone had stabbed them in the back, a fact which explained why they had felt so stiff at the theater.

In a similar vein is the incident related by Dwight Dill, now of Dallas, Texas. He says:

"At the time I was the Election Judge for the wet and dry vote, and I cannot just remember as to whether I sent both of the Willkie boys to jail or whether only one, but I am inclined to believe both of them were in on this rumpus. The News of that date will disclose, I think, that the Willkie boys were not satisfied with the election and so they came down to my house in force, that is with three or four hundred students, and staged a demonstration. That night John Harris, who was Mayor, called me and said that the boys from the forks of the creek were assembled up town and getting ready to clean out the students, and I went up and mingled with them at his suggestion, and we finally talked them out of any disorder. However, that was a wild time, for the next morning the Willkie boys started a petition at the University asking for my resignation but Dr. Bryan put an end to this movement and everything eventually smoothed up."

In spite of all the activities (and studies were never neglected), Wendell found time, when the daughter of one of his Elwood friends had difficulties in finding a room when her rooming house was closed, to stop everything until she was suitably located. Because Captain Nuzum was well acquainted with military maneuvers, the Willkie boys used to undergo a severe examination at his hands whenever they came home. They never, even to this day, although their lives have led them far away from Elwood, have forgotten the friends of their boyhood days. Shortly before his graduation Wendell brought to Elwood a friend who expected to begin his professional life here. The latter engaged a house with the understanding that he was to pay a certain sum for the time the house was held vacant for him. When he finally arrived, he decided not to take the house and refused to pay the sum agreed upon. Since Wendell had told the owner that his friend would pay, he felt under obligation and paid the amount himself.

The 1913 *Arbutus* gives as honors and activities other than those that have been discussed his membership on the Interclass Athletic Committee and the Executive Committee of the Student Council. He was also a member of Phi Delta Phi, honorary law fraternity, and of Sigma Delta Rho, honorary debating fraternity.

As during his high school years, school vacations were no times for idleness. One summer he went to Oklahoma and followed the wheat harvest northward. He was a barker for a tent lodging house in South Dakota during a boom, bringing drunks who had not foreseen the need of a lodging and keeping the place filled at fifty cents a head; a migratory farm hand in California; a laborer in a steel mill; and a short order cook and waiter. These were not only means of securing money, they were excursions into the real world which kept his class work from

Talking It Over With Repair Crew of Ohio Edison

Camp De Souge, France

being too academic and which gave his studies a setting in reality. On one of his visits home, he helped his father defend and win a case for some labor picketers against whom an injunction had been issued.

Deciding to become a Mason, he studied for his degrees under the direction of Mayor Brumbaugh. He took his first degree April 1, 1913; his second September 5, 1913; and his third September 9, 1913. His old friend O. D. (Doc) Hinshaw conducted his initiation into these degrees. He retained his membership in the Elwood lodge until May 18, 1920, when he took a demit and became a charter member of Coventry Lodge 665, F. & A. M., at Akron.

The next fall after graduating from Indiana University, he went to Coffeyville, Kansas, to teach history. In addition he coached a track team which won all its meets. He had never played basketball, but he studied the game and turned out a team that won six of its ten games. He coached a girls' basketball team, organized debate teams, sponsored the school's Hi-Y club, and advised the literary society. It is no wonder, then that the Coffeyville annual in the spring featured Mr. Willkie. The annual cartooned him as a huge pepperbox haranguing an empty auditorium.

He was engaged to teach in Coffeyville for a second year; but his brother Fred had a position with the Fajardo Sugar Company at Fajardo, Porto Rico, and Wendell wanted him to secure a position for him there. When he received word of his brother's success, he resigned his position at Coffeyville (December 14, 1914) and went to Oberlin College and took a special course in spectrum analysis to fit him for his work there. He kept this position just for a summer.

When he returned to college to complete his law education, he seemed much changed. Of course, being a graduate, he was unable to take part in the undergraduate affairs. He had been off the campus for two years, and nowhere does the population change faster than in a college. He spent most of his spare time in the clubrooms of Phi Delta Phi, the honorary law fraternity, discussing law problems with other law students. He did attend the Socialist Club for the opportunities it gave him for debate and was one of the Extension Debaters in 1916. His disconcerting commencement experience has already been recounted.

Somewhere about this time occurred a memorable experience with an automobile. A taxi driver in Elwood had an Overland touring car that had seen long usage. During fair weeks, it had carried as many as twenty passengers to and from the fair grounds. Wendell and two of the other Willkie boys engaged the owner of the car to take them to Winamac. Everything that could happen to a car happened on this trip. When they got back, the owner put the car in good condition again for his business.

Some time later, Robert, Wendell, and Fred wanted to go to Lake Barbee and asked to rent this car. When the owner asked them if they could drive, they evaded the question but left him with the mistaken impression that they could. When they got safely to Wabash without a mishap, they were so pleased that they sent him a telegram. The trip was completed without a mishap;

and, not long after their return, Robert, his father, and some say Wendell bought the car for $250.

Wendell, however, never made a good driver. He was too full of argumentation and could not argue without using his hands freely. Horses will keep the road when no one holds the reins—some horses—but automobiles will not. After one experience of that sort, Wendell decided that he was not born to drive an auto-mobile.

SETTLING DOWN

On the completion of his law course, Wendell returned to Elwood to practice law with his father. By that time, his brother Robert was deputy prosecuting attorney. One day, Robert had a case which was to be tried before the justice of the peace court at Frankton, in the southern part of the county. Wendell induced him to turn the case over to him. When he arrived at Frankton, he was recognized; and Doctor Harold, a veterinary surgeon, a friend of Wendell's, helped to cook up a hoax for the unsuspecting lawyer. One of the partners in the plot impersonated the bailiff and brought Doctor Harold to the courtroom. The doctor asked Wendell if he were the one who was to try the case. When Wendell told him that he was to prosecute the case, the doctor looked down his nose and said lugubriously, "Well, Wendell, be as easy on me as you can." At this, the prosecutor thought that he had made the trip to Frankton to prosecute one of his good friends; and he was considerably set back. After carrying on the joke for some time, the perpetrators could hold in no longer. Wendell said that he had decided that he would resign rather than prosecute his friend.

About this time occurred an event of much importance in Wendell's life. One of his friends, who had spent the summer with him at Culver in 1906, was about to marry a young woman in Rushville, Indiana; and, he asked Wendell to serve as an usher at the wedding. On this occasion, he met for the first time Miss Edith Wilk. She had been in the class of 1913 at Indiana University but had dropped out at the end of her sophomore year.

Various romantic tales have been told of what happened next. Evidently they made a good impression upon each other. An item in the minutes of the board of the Elwood library read: "Sept. 5, 1916. Chairman reported that a Miss Wilk of Rushville, Indiana would accept the position of librarian here at $65.00 a month. The com. reported that Miss Wilk had one year at Butler and one year at Bloomington—and a summer course in library work—was a pleasing personality."

There are rather substantial rumors that Wendell Willkie, who had very good friends on the board was instrumental in having the offer made to Miss Wilk. Be that as it may, Miss Wilk did accept the position; and one of the frequent visitors at the library was the book-loving Wendell Willkie. Across the street from the library was at that time a vacant lot. Wendell was making a political speech one day in the regular Willkie style, voice booming, hands going like a windmill—when he suddenly saw that Miss Wilk had come out to the steps of the library to listen. The effect was miraculous.

142

One auditor says that the effect was as if an automobile was going at full speed and suddenly ran out of gas.

On November 14, 1916, the library minutes report that the president asked for a report on success in obtaining a new librarian, as Miss Wilk was intending to go home as soon as one could be found. Various stories have connected her departure with her relations with Mr. Willkie. However, she had come to the Elwood library with the understanding that she should stay only until a well-qualified librarian could be secured permanently and not with any intention of staying. All reports that her departure was due to the presence of Mr. Willkie on the board are unfounded, because the minutes of the board show that he was not a member of the board until January 9, 1917, about six weeks after Miss Wilk left Elwood.

Miss Wilk's ancestors on her mother's side were Scotch-Irish who came to this country before the Revolution. Her father's father came to this country from Germany while he still wore long clothes. Mr. Wilk was a construction engineer and for some time was stationed at Nashville, Tennessee, where his two daughters Edith and Erema were born. When Edith was seven years old, the family returned to Rushville, which they had always considered their home. Mr. Wilk supervised the construction of the courthouse at Rushville and of the road which runs past the largest of Mr. Willkie's farms.

At Indiana University, Edith became a member of the Kappa Alpha Theta Sorority. She was very pretty and was very popular among the young men at Rushville and

Bloomington and at Indianapolis, where she frequently visited. Library work, however, appealed to her more than any of the young men she had seen; so she worked in the library at Rushville and Elwood but then returned to Rushville, not quite so certain that she wanted to be a librarian.

On May 10, a day, as will be seen, easily remembered, Robert and Wendell went to Frankfort to plead in a justice of the peace court in a suit for damages growing out of an automobile accident. The suit was for $50; but, as the case progressed, they amended their complaint several times. Although they had told their client that they thought his suit was hopeless, the trial resulted in a verdict of $150 in his favor.

War

On the day that the news flashed across the country that war had been declared, Wendell Willkie enlisted as a private. He and his brother Robert went to the first Reserve Officers' Training Camp at Fort Benjamin Harrison, Indiana, May 11, 1917.

Up to this time, he had gone under the name given him by his parents—Lewis Wendell Willkie. By a clerical error, his name was recorded as Wendell Lewis Willkie. (It may be remembered that Ulysses Simpson Grant owed his name to a similar error at West Point.) When he called attention to the error, he was told that the war would probably be over before the error could be corrected. Since he had never liked the name *Lewis*, he was satisfied to have it buried in the middle of his name and reduced it to the initial. Since that time, he

144

has used the name by which he is now known—Wendell L. Willkie.

On August 14, he was sent to Camp Zachary Taylor, Kentucky. He had been appointed First Lieutenant, Infantry, O.R.C., but was assigned to the 325th Field Artillery (84th Division), in spite of the fact that his training had been in the infantry. It has been suggested that, since his name began with W, the requirements of the infantry had been filled before the officers got to his name. In a short time, he was sent to Fort Sill, Oklahoma, where he received instruction in firing and in balloon work. He became a balloon observer and was sent to Harvard University for special training.

Sometime during these events, Miss Wilk had agreed to add a syllable to her name; and the wedding date was set for a day in January, 1918. Mr. Willkie secured a furlough so that he might attend his wedding, but he was caught in the memorable blizzard during that eventful winter, and his train was stalled in the snow twenty-five miles from Rushville. The roads were impassable; but he did manage to get to a telephone, by means of which he was able to keep in touch with her over Saturday, Sunday, and Monday.

She had telephoned to him to bring her wedding bouquet with him from Louisville; and, when he did finally arrive on Monday, he still had it—frozen. The wedding was held in the old Wilk homestead in Rushville, January 14, 1918. She was dressed in white satin and wore a veil—and carried the frozen bouquet of white orchids and lilies-of-the-valley. After their marriage, Mrs. Willkie made her home in New Albany during Wendell's stay at Camp Taylor, Louisville.

On June 15, 1918, his organization was moved to West Point, Kentucky; and, on September 9, 1918, he sailed overseas on *S. S. Canada*. After disembarking at Le Havre, the regiment went to Camp De Souge. Since the armistice was signed a month later, he did not see any active service. He did see some of France. In due course, as a result of his excellent record, he was promoted to a captaincy. Expecting to return to the practice of law in this country and feeling a natural sympathy for the men, he represented enlisted men who got into court-martial scrapes over matters which he thought were of slight importance. He returned from overseas on the *S. S. Antigone*, February 15, 1919. Mrs. Willkie met him at the pier.

On July 22, 1940, forty members of the 325th Regiment met at Kokomo, Indiana, to make preliminary arrangements for taking part on the occasion of the acceptance speech. Representatives of all the batteries of the 325th Regiment had previously met and elected Mr. Willkie honorary president. The 325th Field Artillery band will be on hand to lead the regiment. Naturally, the conversation turned to the time when they were in the army. Henry L. Myers, who was battery clerk in Willkie's battery, recalls that soon after a large number of ths smen had been sent to Hattiesburg, Mississippi, word came that there was to be an inspection. There were only Willkie, the clerk, the cook, and two or three others there. Everything was in confusion from the

146

Mess at Camp De Souge, France

The REGIMENT IS PROUD of YOU.
325th F.A.

Ryan.

They Remember Willkie

departure of the others. Willkie announced that the place would have to be cleaned up.

"Who'll do it?" Myers asked.

"Why, we will," Willkie replied, rolling up his sleeves and setting to work.

They got the place in spic and span order just as the inspectors reached the unit before theirs.

B. Good, of Peru, was mess sergeant in Battery F. He said that Willkie used to come into the kitchen every morning and read the morning paper. Then they would chat for a while. He recalled Willkie as a jovial, friendly officer.

Several recalled that, when an enlisted man got in trouble, he could ask any officer to help him before the court-martial. Willkie, they said, was called on by the privates more than any other of the officers.

Paul Miller, of Indianapolis, said that he would always remember his experience with Willkie. At his first roll call, Willkie ordered him to step forward. He wondered what he had done, but Willkie wanted to know if it was true that he had had military training at Purdue. When he replied that it was, he was ordered back into the ranks. A week later, Willkie made him a corporal, saying that more noncommissioned men were needed and that his training qualified him for the advance.

William Arnold, of Peru, told about being represented by Willkie at a court-martial for being out at a dance beyond his time. This time, Willkie was unsuccessful, and Sergeant Arnold was broken for thirty days and given K. P. duty.

The character of Lieutenant Willkie was shown by an incident told by O. W. Robbins, of Twelve Mile, Indiana. He was connected with the schools in the encampment and one day entered the headquarters building when someone in an adjoining room was getting a dressing down. The walls were thin, and he could not help hearing what was said. The colonel was telling Willkie in no uncertain terms that he was too familiar with the enlisted men and that he must stop it.

"Nothing doing," Willkie replied. "I am associating every day with men I'd be proud to look up to in private life."

Several of the men told about his contempt of the distinctions between officers and men. They might be sitting around talking when they would hear someone call out, "It's just me. Sit still;" and then Lieutenant Willkie would come from around the corner.

One of the proudest recollects of Henry Sherrard, of near Kokomo, is the praise given him by Willkie. When their ship docked at Glasgow, an inspection was held before the men disembarked. When Willkie came to him, he looked at his pack, held it up for all to see, and told the men that that was the neatest pack he had seen and told them to try to make theirs like it.

One of the duties of the officers was to censor the letters sent by the men while they were abroad. Mrs. Sherrard still has the letters Mr. Sherrard wrote her, and they are marked "Censored by W. L. Willkie". Mr. Sherrard had on exhibit recently at Kokomo Mr. Willkie's gas mask. The officers' masks were just like the men's, so that the Germans could not recognize the officers and kill them. After the Armistice, orders came to turn in all gas masks by November 21, 1918. Later, orders came that the men might retain their masks and their steel helmets as souvenirs. Many did not claim theirs; but Hugh Enyeart, of Hoover, Indiana, picked out Willkie's and kept it. The name W. L. *Willkie* had been written on it in three-inch letters, apparently with an indelible pencil. Mr. Enyeart lent the mask to Mr. Sherrard.

The common remark of the men at this reunion was "We're Wendell Willkie's outfit, and we're proud of him."

He was honorably discharged at Camp Sherman, Ohio, February 28, 1919. He was now faced with the problem of establishing himself in his profession. Those who had remained at home during the war had found the years prosperous and had, naturally, fitted themselves into the affairs of the community. Those returning from the army, especially those who had been abroad, found plenty of kind words but few openings. With the slack resulting from the cessation of hectic operations of the wartime economy, there appeared to be a discouraging lack of opportunity. This was directly noticeable, of course, in regard to positions in stores, offices, and factories, which had, in patriotic fervor, promised that their old positions would be waiting for the soldiers when they came home. When the time came, however, this was not easy to do, even when the employers honestly desired to fulfill their pledges. For the professional man, the situation was no less, perhaps it was more, difficult. During the two years of absence, associations had been made by possible clients, associations not easily broken or changed.

Akron

Returning to Elwood with his wife, Wendell Willkie established his law office anew and set about the always discouraging task of building up a legal practice. Before the end of 1919, he had an opportunity to enter the legal department of the Firestone Tire and Rubber Company at Akron, Ohio. Here was a problem: Should he continue his efforts to establish a legal practice for himself or should he merge himself in a legal department of a large corporation? And there was the associated problem of whether he should leave the region which he knew so well and where he was so well known and go to a city where his arrival and his activities would hardly be noted. The position at Akron guaranteed him $150 a month at the start; to stay at Elwood was to run the usual risks of the legal aspirant, but he would be free to follow his own bent and to win such fortune as his ability might deserve. He put the question to his wife, who assured him that whatever he decided would meet her approval. He talked the matter over with his good friends in Elwood. "We're going to Akron," he announced to his wife one day—a momentous decision, the turning point in his career.

So, late in 1919, with hardly a ripple, Wendell Willkie entered the life of Akron. It was not long, however, until the ripples began to appear. Mr. Willkie became fascinated with corporation law. He was full of vitality, able to read—and he did—until two o'clock in

Earl Ryan, Chef de Gare of 40 and 8 Club, Des Moines, Gives Willkie American Legion Button

Register News Bureau.

Lieutenant Willkie—1918

the morning and, after two hours' sleep, get up and read until breakfast. (When he could not afford bookcases, he followed his parents' example of buying books and piled them about on the floor.) He frequently worked fifteen to eighteen hours a day. His pre-occupation with his work made him careless about his appearance, much to the concern of his professional associates—but he won cases!

By 1921, he had attracted the attention of Mather and Nesbitt, a law firm which represented many large railroad, industrial, banking, and utility companies in northeastern Ohio and became the junior partner of Mather, Nesbitt & Willkie. Influenced by the years of association with his father, who had never been able to turn down an opportunity to represent workmen or labor groups, Mr. Willkie often surprised the utility companies which he might be representing on some major case by appearing against them in personal damage suits brought by their workmen.

During the eight years of his association with Mather, Nesbitt & Willkie, the business of the firm increased threefold. Growing out of his interests with the firm, he became a stockholder and director of the Ohio State Bank at Akron.

About this time, the Ku Klux Klan had secured an influence over the schools at Akron which seemed to many to endanger their success. Mr. Willkie, son of the Willkies of Elwood, could not be indifferent to this danger. Besides, his son, Philip, had been born (December 7, 1919) shortly after Mr. Willkie's arrival at Akron; and freedom in the schools has naturally been a matter of concern to him ever since. From 1924 to 1926, he led the fight against the Klan's influence and succeeded in freeing the schools from this danger.

In 1922, Wendell, Robert, and Fred Willkie were still members of the Louis Monroe Post 53 of the American Legion. However, Wendell helped organize Summit Post No. 19 in Akron and served two terms as its commander. He became interested in politics and considered running for congress, but a friend told him that he would have the misfortune to be elected and that that would end his career. He became a personal friend of Governor James M. Cox, of Michigan, Democratic candidate for the presidency in 1920. In 1924, at the request of Governor Cox, he was a delegate to the 1924 Democratic Convention, where he opposed the nomination of William Gibbs McAdoo. He had little more to do with politics until the campaign of 1932, when he supported Newton D. Baker for the presidency.

COMMONWEALTH & SOUTHERN

Meanwhile, Mr. Willkie went on winning cases at law for the corporations represented by his firm. One of these corporations was the Ohio Edison Company. About this time something was going on in financial and utilities circles which was destined to be of great importance to Mr. Willkie. In May, 1929, Bonbright & Company, Incorporated, of New York, an investment firm, secured large interests in the Commonwealth Power Corporation, the Southern Power and Light Company, and the Penn-Ohio Edison Company. Later, the Consumers Power Company, the Central Illinois Light Company, the Southern Indiana Gas and Electric Company, the Ohio Edison Company, the Pennsylvania Power Company, the Alabama Power Company, the Georgia Power Company, the Gulf Power Company, the Mississippi Power Company, and the South Carolina Power Company were all organized under the Commonwealth and Southern Corporation as the top holding company, making this one of the three largest electric systems in the country.

The assets of this system wre over one and an eighth billion dollars. In 1929, the system consisted of 165 companies divided into two groups, the Northern and Southern. Between 1929 and 1939, 57 other companies were taken into the system; but, in harmony with the policy recommended by the Government, this system had been reduced by the beginning of 1940 to 40 companies; and, by the end of this year, there will be only 33. This system furnished electricity, gas, transportation, and other utilities to more than 3500 communities in eleven industrial and farming states. More than four-fifths of its revenue came from the sale of electricity and about half of the remainder from the sale of gas.

Perhaps it would be well to explain the general nature of a holding company. Ever since the publicity given holding companies by the crash of the Insull empire, there has been a general impression that there must be something intrinsically wrong with such organizations. The holding company is one which controls the voting stock of another or other companies. Those who are friendly to such organizations argue that they increase efficiency by bringing about unity between interconnected systems, decreasing overlapping expenditures, help to supply them capital, and furnish valuable assistance in management. Those who are unfriendly to them have invested them with all the wiles of the evil one. As Mr. Willkie has repeatedly said, business concerns are not good nor bad because of their size; they are not good because of their organization. They are good if they operate for the good of their community and country. According to the wording of the law defining holding companies, it is "any company that directly or indirectly owns, controls or holds with power to vote" a specified part of the voting securities of a public utility—"unless the commission, as hereinafter provided, by order declares such a company not a holding company."

This touches upon a point which has aroused Mr. Willkie's ire. Why, he urges, should a commission entrusted with the regulation of the holding companies also be entrusted with the right to determine whether a given company comes under its jurisdiction or not? When the so-called "death sentence" was passed upon holding companies by the law providing for their dissolution by the present year, the Power Commission was granted the power to extend this term for particular companies if it saw fit and even to determine if they might be exempted from the ruling of this law. This, Mr. Willkie argues, makes business subject to discipline, not on the basis of its violation of any law, but upon the prejudices of the commission which is both prosecutor, jury, and judge.

But to return to the organization of the Commonwealth and Southern corporation—As will be seen, the Ohio

Edison Company, for which Mr. Willkie was attorney, was one of the companies absorbed. When Bernard C. Cobb, president of the Commonwealth Power & Penn-Ohio Company, became president of the Commonwealth and Southern, he was not long in noticing the activity of the Ohio Edison's attorney. The story goes that he told Mr. Willkie to figure up his earnings in the last year and promised to double that figure if he would come to New York and serve as attorney for the holding company. Mr. Willkie consequently left Akron and entered the partnership of Weadock & Willkie in New York. By 1933, Mr. Cobb had rid the Commonwealth & Southern of most of the features which have made the holding company objectionable. Desiring to retire from the presidency of the company, he recommended Willkie for the job.

Willkie had been advocating the regulation of holding companies so as to avoid the undesirable features of such companies. Alva Johnston in the *Saturday Evening Post* tells of a meeting between Willkie and Insull in 1929, at a meeting of utility executives. This was at the time that Insull was the utility king of the nation. Insull was bitter about the attacks of the "radicals" against his policies and wanted the talk stopped. Willkie was in favor of everyone saying what he wished on the ground that unjustified criticism would destroy itself and justified criticism was good for all. With a positive air of superiority, Insull told that he would know better when he got older. Mr. Willkie saw to it that bankers were removed from the board of the Commonwealth and Southern and did away with the office of chairman of the board. When he was offered a raise in salary, he replied that his salary of $75,000 a year was as great as that of the president of the United States and that was enough.

When he found himself at the age of forty-one at the head of this immense organization, the depression was at its depth. The income of the utilities both from services and from equipment were low and dropping lower. Salesmen were being laid off in order to save money. Holding to the idea a generation before held by his father that wide distribution and low rates was the solution to the utilities problem, he launched a sales campaign. More than 500 salesmen were hired and put to work to sell electrical devices upon liberal credit terms. To encourage the use of these appliances, he set up a plan by which the housewife consumer, after using a certain amount of electricity, could get an additional one-third of this amount free. Not content to sit in his office while others pushed his ideas, he went about to every part of the region served by his company, making personal contacts that might lead to the increased sale of electrical equipment and so, ultimately, of electricity. As a result, he doubled the average domestic use of electricity in his territory and cut the domestic rates in half.

When he found this plan successful, he took the risk that he had hesitated to take before. Since 1933, he has reduced the consumer costs of electricity 41% and increased consumption 83%. On January 6, 1938, he met Attorney General Robert H. Jackson on the Town Hall of the Air program on the topic "How can Government and Business Work Together". In answer to the argument that the large utility companies were responsible for high rates and that the small companies brought low rates, Mr. Willkie called attention to the fact that every state in the union had independent utilities and also utilities affiliated with holding companies and that in forty-four of these states, the rates of the latter were less than those of the independent companies. He held that there was something amusing in the spectacle of government officials telling big business the desirability of low price and large volume, since this was a technique that big business had developed through mass production and distribution. He cited the achievements in this direction made by the oil companies, the telephone companies, and the automobile manufacturers. "Since the prewar years," he said, "the cost of living has gone up about 40%, and the cost of electricity in this country has gone down by almost exactly the same percent. The American consumer pays a smaller part of his income for electricity than the consumers in any country in Europe."

The achievements of the young president of Commonwealth & Southern might have passed unmarked had it not come before the public in connection with his fight against the TVA. About the time he became president of the Commonwealth & Southern, the Tennessee Valley Authority was created. His company had large interests in Tennessee and Mississippi, where the Government began its experiment. Willkie opposed the plan and called attention to the fact that the electric rates in his territory were cheaper than those offered by any other company in the country.

He still calls himself a La Follette liberal, but he has clashed with the younger La Follettes on the question of utilities. He very simply explains the apparent conflict that the La Follettes point out. Robert La Follette, he says, fought "against the domination of the legislature, the courts, and the people by big business. Today there is the same struggle—against domination of the legislature, the courts, and the people by big government." He quotes Thomas Edison: "There is far more danger in public monopoly than there is in private monopoly, for when the government goes into business it can shift its losses to the taxpayers. If it goes into the power business it can pretend to sell cheap power and then cover up its losses. The government never really goes into business, for it never makes ends meet, and that is the first requisite of business. It just mixes a little business with a lot of politics and no one ever gets a chance to find out what is actually going on."

Perhaps the situation in the Tennessee Valley from Mr. Willkie's point of view can be explained by reference to the situation which prompted the trust busting of the Theodore Roosevelt era. By means of railroad rebates, the big companies were able to enter competitive territory and underbid their competitors. They established two sets of prices, one, often below cost, for territories where they had competition and for other regions a price sufficiently high to recoup them for their losses in the former. They influenced the legislatures both to prevent adverse action against them and to grant them unjustified favors. As a result, the liberal element in America made common cause against them.

Such were some of the sins of big business which La Follette opposed. Today, however, it is government which goes into competitive territory and slashes rates. The system of bookkeeping by which these rates are justified is one which the government would never permit the utilities to employ. Since the government does not pay taxes, it has a virtual rebate as effective as any the railroads gave the Standard Oil Company in the days when big business held the reins over the government. By its unlimited credit resources, the government can continue even when deficits pile up; but private utilities can not do this.

One point in regard to such competition in the case of utilities is the fact that, by nature, public utilities are natural monopolies. That is, to take an evident case, it would be a waste of money for two water companies to lay their pipes in the city streets to supply the same district. The cost to each would be the same, but each would receive, under the most favorable conditions, half the income which a single company would receive. The same is true of telephone lines, gas lines, street car lines, and electric lines. Consequently, almost without exception, competition between such utilities is rare and uneconomical.

Mr. Willkie pointed out this fact in his own cogent way and insisted that the TVA should not set up competing lines. If it wished to enter the territory then served by an existing utility, it should buy out this utility rather than duplicate the equipment and impoverish both of them. He then began to deal with the TVA for the purchase of the Tennessee Electric Power Company, the

Commonwealth & Southern property in the area entered by the TVA.

At the time, this was a bold step. The temper of the country was favorable to the New Deal activities. The Muscle Shoals structures had been a white elephant for the nation ever since the close of the World War and had aroused great bitterness both against the government and against big business, and the Tennessee Valley Authority seemed to be the logical solution to this problem. Mr. Willkie's stand against the government was considered a stand against the whole New Deal. Business men had come to feel that the best thing to do was to acquiesce in government regulation until there was a change in public opinion. But Mr. Willkie would not take their advice and remain silent. That was not the Willkie way. As a result, he became a frequent visitor to governmental hearings, where he spoke out in a way that made other business heads tremble.

The government offered $67,000,000 for the Tennessee Electric Power holdings; Willkie insisted on over $90,-000,000. After numerous hearings, Mr. Willkie suggested that the Securities and Exchange Commission arbitrate the matter. This offer was agreed upon, and the TVA and the communities which under its direction were setting up their own electric and power systems gave on August 15, 1939, after a six-year battle, checks for a total of $78,600,000 in full payment for the Tennessee Electric & Power Company. As he received the checks, Mr. Willkie remarked. "That's a lot of money for an Indiana farmer to be kicking around." This was about $7,500,000 less than Mr. Willkie considered a fair valuation for the properties, but it made possible full payment of bonds and preferred stock at par and left about $8,000,000 for Commonwealth & Southern, owner of all but a few shares of the common stock.

During the six years that this contest with the TVA had been going on, Mr. Willkie had been doing something else. In 1934, the company had a loss of $1,600,000. Preferred stock dividends had accumulated to $16.50 a share. He had reduced the company's rates until they were 27% below the average for the United States.

While an attorney in Akron, he had represented the utility company for years in a rate dispute with Akron. He believed that it was not good policy to be constantly fighting one's customers about rates. When he became president of the Commonwealth & Southern, he at once set about the task of ending such conflicts. In 1937, his company had made a profit of $10,600,000; in 1938, the company earned $10,204,848; and, in 1939, it earned $13,413,636. He had become chairman of the board of the Consumers Power Company and the Ohio Edison Company and director of the Central Illinois Light Company, the Southern Indiana Gas and Electric Company, and other utility corporations.

But he had done something else of great importance. He had convinced a great number of people of his ability, his sincerity, and his honesty. David Lilienthal, of the TVA admitted that he "has done a real job of selling electricity at low rates." Various members of the Administration expressed admiration for his conduct.

This brings his career to another crisis. Financially, he had prospered. He had a fortune that has been estimated at around half a million dollars. He still retained many of the manners of his early years; he still likes to put his feet on his desk, is indifferent about his food and his clothes, still likes to read. He has read extensively—and intensively—in English history of the South and of Indiana, in the history of trade unions, socialism, communism, and other movements. His library of about 2,500 books is made up of the old masters, of modern literature, of books on economics, sociology, war, and the New Deal—books bought for use. Recently, he reviewed for the New York "Herald," *The Young Melbourne, and the Story of His Marriage with Caroline Lamb.* His recreations are playing poker, reading, talking, and visiting his farms.

He and his wife and son are members of the Episcopal Church. He is a member in New York of the Century, University, Recess, Lawyers, and Blind Brook clubs. His business address is 20 Pine Street, New York City.

THE WILLKIE FARMS

Six years ago, disturbed by the economic uncertainties of the times, Mr. Willkie looked about for some safe investment to take care of his family. His research department examined various investments to determine which in the past had best withstood the vicissitudes of governmental and economic changes. It reported that farm land had come through all kinds of conditions with less depreciation and with more certain profit than any other investment.

So, he looked about for a good farm investment. He finally authorized Mrs. Willkie's father, Philip Wilk, to purchase for him a 363-acre tract in Walker Township, Rush County. This tract is somewhat hilly for that region and includes a wooded tract and considerable pasture as well as tillable land. The present tenants have lived on the farm for eighteen years. Since Mr. Willkie purchased it, the barn has been remodeled and painted (The barns on all his farms are painted Big Four yellow, the popular color for barns in that section), cattle barns have been built, and the house has been painted. There are several driven wells on the farm, and the well in the wooded tract is an open flowing well. At present, a lot of Hereford cattle from Texas but purchased in Indianapolis are being fed for the market.

This, and the other farms purchased by Mr. Willkie, was bought as an investment, not as a hobby or luxury. However, he soon became attached to the farm. He loves to see things grow and remarked once while watching some cattle on one of his farms, "I could look at them all day." For several years he has visited his farms almost once a month, often riding long distances and sometimes flying so that he might do so. Nothing seems to give him more pleasure than to see the growth of a litter of pigs since his last visit.

He soon bought a 398-acre tract about four miles northwest of Rushville. A number of wells have been driven in this farm. On this farm are five gas wells, which have long been leased to a gas company with headquarters at Newcastle. Naturally, the house is supplied with gas from these wells.

Two other farms near this one, one of 289 acres and one of 141 acres across the road from each other and a short distance from the second farm were also purchased. His most recent purchase was a farm adjoining the rear of the 289-acre farm.

When purchased, these farms were run down, and the buildings were in need of repair. One of the farms had been taken over by an insurance company. Mr. Wilk, Mrs. Willkie's father, gave up his position as a book-keeper in Rushville to manage these farms for him. Upon his death, Miss Mary Sleeth, a girlhood friend of Mrs. Willkie, and librarian at the Rushville library when Mrs. Willkie was assistant librarian there, took over this work. Mr. Willkie remarked to her once that he would be ashamed if a farm deteriorated while in his possession.

Consequently, his aim so far has been to restore them to good condition. Since the farms were bought for business reasons, he has expected them to make a profit; and they have averaged a net profit of about three per-cent ever since he has owned them. This profit, how-ever, has been turned back into the farms just as he turned bach the profits of the Commonwealth and Southern for some years to increase its efficiency. Fences have been rebuilt, good gates set up, necessary buildings constructed, and all buildings painted. Wells have been driven wherever they would be of advantage. With a great fondness for trees, more than two hundred ash and elm trees have been set out. His preference, how-ever, is beech trees; and a considerable number of these are being grown for distribution on his farms.

Practically everything produced on the soil remains on the farms. Some wheat is sold, partly to give the tenants ready money, but chiefly because there is insufficient storage room. The other grains are fed, and the wheat and oat straw is used for bedding the cattle and horses and for roughage.

Mr. Willkie's tenants work on a fifty-fifty basis. They furnish their own horses, tractors, and tools; finance half the livestock; and receive half the income. He made the original advance for feeder stock and other stock. They are not required to pay for the feed for their horses nor to pay for the privilege of keeping them, as these requirements, made by some farm owners, tend to work hardships on the tenants; but Mr. Willkie has always, say the tenants, been very fair and helpful in such matters. Last year, one of the tenants found that his hog production had been so much greater than normal that he would be unable to fatten them and so would have to sell them too early for profit. When Mr. Willkie learned this, he financed the purchase of additional feed.

Mud Creek, a stream that never goes dry, flows through all of the farms. It gives the cattle a good wading and drinking place and the boys good fishing, but it is too shallow for swimming.

On his latest purchase, made last year, there was also a shortage of corn; and corn was purchased to fatten the hogs. This is unusual, however. Mr. Willkie is by no means the largest hog-raiser in Rush county, for his general policy is to produce no more hogs than can be fed from the farm itself. Cattle, however, are purchased, pastured, and fed. Most of these are Herefords, and some have been purchased from Kansas City and some from Indianapolis markets.

All of the farms have small herds of dairy cattle, some Herefords, some Guernseys, some Shorthorns, and a few Jerseys. Calves are allowed to run with their mothers in many cases, but there remains a good deal of milking to be done. The whole milk beyond the needs of the tenants is sold to milk processors.

Two sons of one of the tenants won prizes in last year's Rush County Fair for their 4-H Hereford calves and received from Mr. Willkie ten dollars each which he had promised them if they won. They will receive another reward from the presidential candidate if they win ribbons this year, and they are hopeful of qualifying for this.

The year-round hands have their own homes rent free, together with a garden plot. They are given seed and the fruit and berries raised on their plots. They get all the milk they desire, feed for their chickens, and the use of the brooder houses. Their wages are thirty dollars a month.

On most of the farms, pure Hampshire hogs are produced. (Much of the livestock produced on the farms is pure stock, but it is not registered.) On the farm latest purchased, Poland China hogs are raised; and, on the first farm, the hogs are a cross between Hampshire and Duroc stocks. Some sheep are raised.

On all the farms, there is ample pastureland for the cattle; and hay, corn, wheat, and oats are produced. On one farm, barley was raised this year and harvested with a combine; but, as the straw from the wheat and oats

Welcome Home at Akron

"Doc" Hinshaw asks, "Who's Going to Stop Him?"

is needed, these crops are harvested in the typical Indiana way.

Very little beyond what is necessary to keep up the buildings and fences is purchased for the farms. Some feed and minerals and some commercial fertilizer are purchased.

Young orchards have been started on these farms to supply the tenants with fruit, and each tenant has a garden sufficient for his needs. Besides the stock animals, each tenant has a good flock of chickens of the breed that he prefers. Windmills pump water on two of the farms, but they are supplemented by electricity for use when the wind fails. Electricity is used to pump water on two of the other farms and will soon be installed on the remaining farm, where the construction of a new barn and other improvements have been held up by weather conditions and the necessities of tending crops.

All of the tenants have expressed themselves in hearty appreciation of their relations with Mr. Willkie as a landlord. One of them was working on one of Mr. Willkie's farms when the two first met. Mr. Willkie asked him a question, which he answered without stopping his work. Mr. Willkie asked him other questions, which were treated in the same way. After about a quarter-hour of this, Mr. Willkie told him, "I'm going to buy another farm, and I want you to run it for me."

Speaking about this, the tenant said, "Mr. Willkie gave me my chance. If it hadn't been for him, I'd still be doing day labor. Sure Mr. Willkie's a fine man; he gave me my start."

Since his nomination, so many photographers have visited the farm that Miss Sleeth told Mr. Willkie that even the pigs had become camera conscious.

The two most recent tenants have been with him too short a time to have had much contact with the presidential candidate, since he has had little opportunity to visit the farms since last October. Mrs. Wilk, Mrs. Willkie's mother, has been living with her daughter since last fall and so there has not been the same pull to Rushville, and conditions with the Commonwealth & Southern and the many demands on Mr. Willkie for addresses over the country, besides the more recent campaign demands, have made it extremely difficult for him to visit his Rush County holdings.

When asked how Mr. Willkie was able to make a profit from his farms, Miss Sleeth had a ready answer. Nothing takes the place of a good tenant. Mr. Willkie's tenants are efficient and honest. Mr. Willkie will not tolerate a lazy tenant and is very generous with one who does his part. This generosity has, in one way or another, been expressed by the tenants and their wives. The farms are in no way experimental farms nor an idler's fancy, but the best approved farm practices are followed. Instead of marketing live stock in two lots, he spreads his production and sales throughout the year, so minimizing the risks of market fluctuations. Mr. Willkie believes in conservation. Surface erosion is avoided. When he discovered that erosion had started at one point, he was greatly ashamed and took immediate steps to check and prevent it. Soils are analyzed and used to the best advantage. They are fertilized and cropped so as to

maintain and improve their fertility.   Consequently, his
farms have now come to the place where it is no longer
necessary to plow back into them all the new profits;
and an income is being received.

THE GROUNDSWELL

The conflict with the government over the TVA had
begun to make Mr. Willkie known. In 1934, the *Literary
Digest* considered him of national interest and published
his picture.   Early the next year, his speeches began to
be published, and he began to write articles for magazines
of such diverse character as the *Atlantic*, *Fortune*, *Look*,
Saturday Evening Post, and the *New Republic*. From the end
of 1934, the *Reader's Guide* records a continuously growing stream of articles about him—over thirty before
June, 1940.   His picture appeared in *Time*, *Business
Week*, *Newsweek*, *Review of Review*, *Fortune*, and *Life*—it
appeared on the cover of *Time*.   Certainly, he was becoming, if he was not already, a national figure.   His
name appeared frequently in the daily papers.

He began to receive requests to speak at various
gatherings. In two months, according to Hubert Kay in
Life Magazine, he received over two thousand invitations
to speak.   Magazines begged for his articles; publishers
pleaded with him for books.

At the Harvard Club, in New York, after Felix
Frankfurter, justice of the Supreme Court, had addressed several hundred men, an unscheduled discussion
arose between him and Willkie; and the audience stayed
three hours to hear it.   When he was scheduled to speak
before the National Press Club at one of its forum

luncheons, before which some of the most prominent people in the world have spoken, he drew its largest crowd—479 persons—and won their hearty applause.

Before the National Association of Manufacturers at the Waldorf-Astoria Hotel, Mr. Willkie won his audience with his creed:

"I believe in America because in it we are free—free to choose our government, to speak our minds, to observe our different religions;

Because we are generous with those who disagree with us;

Because we hate no people and covet no people's land;

Because we are blessed with a natural and varied abundance;

Because we set no limit to a man's achievements; in mine, factory, field, or service in business or the arts, an able man, regardless of class or creed, can realize his ambition;

Because we have great dreams—and because we have the opportunity to make those dreams come true."

He was invited to meet Robert H. Jackson, Attorney General of the United States in a Town Hall Meeting January 6, 1938. There they discussed *How Can Government and Business Work Together?* Mr. Jackson took the ground that big business was a malefactor which should be opposed by the government in the interests of the public and of the small business man. Mr. Willkie so completely annihilated the argument that little has been heard since of the probability that Mr. Jackson would be a likely presidential candidate. Mr. Willkie pointed out

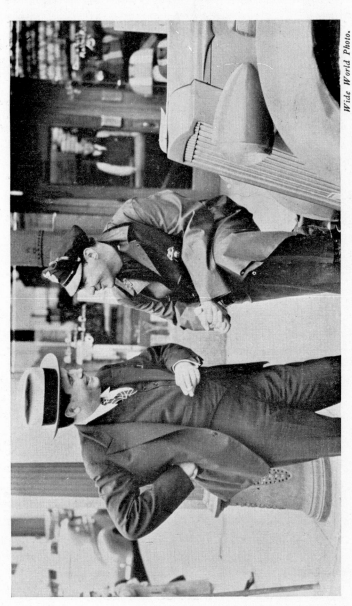

Telling Carl Larsen, Akron Police Officer, "We Need a New Outlook."

Wide World Photo.

Indianapolis Star.

Mrs. Willkie's Mother and Sister Listening to Convention Broadcast

that "Big business supplies a market to small business, not only by buying its products, but by stimulating the general market; moreover, it furnishes small business with low-cost materials and supplies. The two are dependent, one upon the other. When we say that American business is prosperous, we mean that the small businesses of America, which comprise the larger part of our industry, are prosperous." The real cure for depression, he said, "consists in convincing the millions of small investors throughout America that the government does not intend to continue its attack on American industry, big or little, for it is these investors upon whom industry depends for its funds." Then he went on to state the vital problems of government in its relation to business: "modifying restrictions upon buying and selling securities that hamper the investment of funds, readjusting social security laws to a pay-as-you-go basis, protecting rights of both labor and capital in collective bargaining, getting rid of intermediate holding companies in the utility field without declaring death sentence on them."

He appeared on the "Information Please" program, an undertaking to give one pause. Here he matched his wits against the experts—and came out of the ordeal with the heightened respect of the experts and the radio audience.

Mr. Willkie returned to Indiana University to speak at the Foundation Day exercises May 4, 1938. This time, there was no question as to his merits; and he received the degree of Doctor of Laws from his alma mater. Speaking on *The Spirit of Liberalism*, he remarked

179

that "Liberalism is an attitude of mind rather than a fixed program." Emphasizing individual freedom, he said, "I am convinced that there is no possibility for continuing prosperity for the great mass of people except in a free political society and under a free, if supervised, economy."

President Emeritus William Lowe Bryan said as he introduced Mr. Willkie at the Indiana University Foundation Day Banquet that evening at the Claypool Hotel, Indianapolis, Indiana:

"Wendell Willkie reminds me of Theodore Roosevelt. He looks like that Roosevelt. He has the same stocky powerful body. He has the same masterful intelligence which is at the same time masterful will. We are very proud of our boys who run and win along with the best in the world. How proud we are of our men like Willkie who can stand up and fight along with or against the strongest. Roosevelt, the First, would have taken Wendell Willkie to his heart. When Roosevelt, the Second, meets Willkie, he knows that he has met a man. Moreover—you may not know this—as often with a great fighter, this realist is also at heart an idealist."

A year later, May 7, 1940, the president of the National American Woman Suffrage Association presented its gold medal for "distinguished service to humanity" to Mrs. Carrie Chapman Catt, writer, historian, and lecturer who was a leader in the movement for woman's suffrage; to James E. West, chief Scout executive of the Boy Scouts of America; and to Wendell Willkie.

Something was surging up in the consciousness of the nation. Here was a man who was listened to, a man who had something to say that struck sympathetic chords with the faith of his fellow citizens, a man who was not afraid to speak what might be the unpopular thing and was, perhaps, surprised to find that it was popular, a man of faith in the destiny of his nation. In a time when there seemed to be pessimism in government, here was a voice of encouragement.

When a man has arrived at distinction, there is no dearth of those who are ready to take credit for his achievement and to say, "I did it" or "I told you so." So there are more than one claimant to the honor of starting the Willkie boom for the presidency. The fact is that the boom was started by Mr. Willkie himself— by being himself. Others came into the picture only after the public had already become Willkie-conscious. About three years ago, Edward E. Whiting, a New England columnist, expressed the view in his column that Wendell Willkie was the man to be the next president of the United States; but the remark brought no response. About a year ago, several other columnists mentioned him as a possibility; but still there was no reaction. Hugh S. Johnson said that, if he were nominated, he would be a strong candidate and would be a great president. When this was reported to Mr. Willkie, he remarked, "If the government keeps on taking my business away at its recent rate, I'll soon be out of work and looking for a job. Johnson's offer is the best I've had yet." Johnson's remark seemed to be timely, and requests to speak came from all parts of the country. Early last April, his appearance on "Information Please" really started people thinking of him as a presidential possibility; but, even late in April, he was not sure that he should consider it.

Lest it might be thought that Elwood was not interested in Willkie's candidacy until it became apparent that he was a strong candidate, let the record speak. On the evening of May 10, 1940, Arthur E. Harrell, an accountant at the G. I. Sellers & Company plant, and Harry Neanover, Secretary of the Elwood Industrial Bureau, composed the following petition:

We, the citizens of Elwood, Indiana, have observed with increasing satisfaction the growth and development of a man who began his life in our city.

We have watched this man rise to a position of leadership through sheer ability and by his own efforts.

We have faith in his ability, his leadership, his integrity and his sound judgment and firmly believe that he is well qualified to direct our nation in the solution of the many problems confronting us today.

We, the citizens of Elwood, Indiana, without regard to political affiliation, stand united in our plea that Wendell L. Willkie, our native son and fellow citizen, shall render himself available as a presidential nominee should this high honor be accorded him by any major political party.

This petition with blanks for signatures, was left at various business houses in Elwood; and, in a short time, over two thousand signatures had been secured.

About the same time, a Willkie-for-President club was formed independently under the leadership of Arthur E. Harrell. Cards after the idea of chain letters were sent out by this organization, and a number of clubs were formed as a result. The Elwood club began to make plans for a rally to be held in the high school gymnasium May 20. Although there were a number of other meetings and banquets scheduled for that night, several hundred people attended the rally. The meeting was preceded by a parade through the main part of the town, led by the senior high school band. Dr. G. V. Newcomer served as master of ceremonies. Talks boosting Mr. Willkie's candidacy were given by a number of prominent citizens, old friends of Wendell Willkie and of his family.

The high light of the evening was a talk by Mr. Willkie himself over a leased wire from his New York home. He expressed his appreciation of the interest shown by his home town and promised that, if he were nominated, he would make his acceptance speech from the steps of the old high school from which he had graduated.

The most remarkable fact about the whole matter is that the activity in behalf of Mr. Willkie seemed spontaneous. It was not engineered by politicians. Oren Root, Jr., great-nephew of Elihu Root, read a magazine article by Mr. Willkie, heard him speak, and began to circulate a chain letter expressing a belief in Mr. Willkie's fitness for the presidency. By April 11, he was receiving so many telephone calls at the law office where he was holding his first position that he was compelled to give up his job and get a new telephone and mail address.

Long before this, *Fortune Magazine* had published an article by Mr. Willkie; and, about time Oren Root was beginning his one-man campaign, the magazine published *We, the People*, with the subtitle *A foundation for a political platform for recovery.* This played such an important part in the campaign for Mr. Willkie's nomination that it is reproduced here. If the reader is interested only in the story of the campaign, he should skip the article for the moment; but it so ably sums up Mr. Willkie's views on a number of important questions that it really amounts to his political platform and deserves careful reading:

MR. WILLKIE'S PETITION

Before the political platforms are written, we, the people, have a declaration and a petition to make.

In the decade beginning 1930 you have told us that our day is finished, that we can grow no more, and that the future cannot be the equal of the past. But we, the people, do not believe this, and we say to you: give up this vested interest that you have in depression, open your eyes to the future, help us to build a New World

In this decade you have separated "business" and "industry" from the ordinary lives of the people and have applied against them a philosophy of hate and mistrust, but, we, the people, say: business and industry are part of our daily lives; in hurting them you hurt us. Therefore abandon this attitude of hate and set our enterprises free.

In this decade you have undertaken vast new obligations, which we support. But because you have not
applied to these obligations the ordinary standards of
business judgment, you have lost our money by the
billions and we, the people, say: give us a businesslike
administration that will act as the steward of our
prosperity; that will ensure the social progress that is
now threatened; and that will manage our affairs at
least as intelligently as we manage our own enterprises.

In this decade, under the banners of reform, you have
usurped our sovereign power by curtailing the Bill
of Rights, by short-circuiting the states, and by placing
in the hands of a few men in executive commissions all
the powers requisite to tyranny; and we, the people,
say to you: we do not want monopolistic government,
any more than we want monopolistic industry. Give
us back the powers that our forefathers declared to be
ours; liberate us to govern ourselves by *law*.

Because you have concealed from us the amount of
our real taxes, and because you have hidden from us
the real nature of our expenditures, you have specifically usurped our power over the public monies, and we,
the people, say: give us as much information concerning our government as we expect to get concerning
our own enterprises, so that we may control the vast
sums that it has become necessary to spend.

You—the politicians of both parties—have muddled
our foreign affairs with politics; with vague threats
and furitive approvals; with wild fears and inconsistent
acts; and we, the people say: give us a foreign policy

that we can trust and upon which we can build toward the future. We are against aggressors; we are for foreign trade; and we recognize that our own standard of living can be improved only by raising the standard of the other countries of the world.

This declaration will not interest those who regard the United States as a laboratory for social experiments.

It will not interest those who regard the United States as a free-lunch counter.

It will certainly not interest those who regard the United States as a somewhat impoverished gold mine out of which they can still scrape a nugget or two for themselves.

It will interest only those who think of the United States as their land—a land that they know and love—a land that became rich through the industry, thrift, and enterprise of its people, and will never regain its prosperity in any other way.   W. L. W.

––––––––––––

WE, THE PEOPLE

A foundation for a political platform for recovery

by Wendell L. Willkie

The American people tend to suspect the structure of political platforms. They know that sometimes these platforms merely glitter with generalities. And they know that sometimes they make specific and important pledges that are subsequently forgotten. The Democratic platform of 1932 was remarkably and creditably

Volunteer Mailing Committee Sending Out Willkie Speeches

Waiting for Convention Hall to Open

specific; yet, in the end, probably no platform was ever more freely repudiated by a successful candidate.

By the same token, the American people tend to suspect political candidates. They know that each is told by his advisers to put on a smile as automatically as a hat, to be photographed going to church, and to play with his grandchildren if he has any — or with somebody else's grandchildren if he hasn't. The candidate should be a fisherman. But above all he must be careful about what he says. If he is talking in the country districts, he should say one thing; in the cities, another. In order to avoid offending this or that pressure group, he may be advised to straddle colossal issues. If he believes in an issue advocated also by his opponent, he is instructed to remain silent lest he give support to the enemy. And should he object to these machinations and try to assert a little independence, he is assured that, once elected, he can ignore all that has gone before.

The American people are not dumb. They know about all this. They know that political platforms are written with the idea of being agreeable to as many different groups of people as possible. They know that all the manifold interests of the U. S. cannot really be satisfied, that the promises to one group will conflict with the promises to another. And the result is that the American people do not give their vote to policies; they give their vote to *men*. They vote for the man who, in their opinion, will not let them down.

The man who will not let them down must be one who understands some fundamental things about them. He must know that they believe in personal integrity — and he must share that belief. He must know that they have a deep and abiding faith in their country — and he must share that faith. He must know that *national* prosperity is more beneficial to them than sectional or occupational prosperity. And he must be the defender of *their* power, and not of the power of any institution or favored group. Such a man's political platform is never written or spoken. It is in his heart and in the hearts of the people.

But while the essence of a great political platform remains always unwritten, it must nevertheless be related as well as possible to contemporary problems and events. Let us consider then, briefly, a platform written for us, not as members of different groups, but as citizens of our great republic; a platform that *we, the people,* should approve. Such a platform would not be political, because it would have to take something from both parties. Indeed, it should not be called a platform at all, but a foundation upon which we can build — not overnight, but slowly — the economic and moral recovery that we have been seeking for so long.

THE NEW WORLD

Before coming to more specific issues it will be well to have a look at the general situation that confronts us — the people — today. It has not as yet been adequately defined by any prominent candidate. And

190

nevertheless its central issue is extremely simple. Its central issue is our power, the people's power, political and economic. The characteristic of our age has been an enormous increase in the power of institutions too big for us to control; power that has been taken out of our hands; power that belongs to us as citizens of a federal democracy. And we conceive that this power must be returned to us if we are to have any hope of resuming in the future the progress that we have made in the past.

It was, as Mr. Roosevelt has indicated, the Republicans who started the trend toward concentration of power. Beginning with the Civil War and gathering headway — chiefly under Republican administrations —until the end of the nineteen-twenties, there grew up a system of private monopolies and quasi monopolies, some beneficial, some ruthless, and all possessing enormous power. This system of industrial monopoly was fostered by a high-tariff policy reaching its apex in the Hawley-Smoot tariff in 1930. Under Republican auspices industrial and financial interests had the favored protection of government. Under Republican auspices, also, the enormous expansion of office space in Washington began.

But the New Deal's answer to this great increase in the power of private monopolies and quasi monopolies has been an even greater increase in the power of government. The New Deal, as we shall see, has extended government power far beyond the limits carefully worked out by the founders of our system. For the old American principle that government is a *liability* to be borne by the citizens for the sake of peace, order, and security, the New Deal has substituted the notion that government is an *asset* without which none of us can survive. With its commissioners, its economists, and its confidential advisers behind unmarked doors, all of whom have power (written *and* unwritten) over our enterprises, the New Deal has gone back to the concept of huge, centralized government — the only concept that men had had before our forefathers sat down and figured out the laws of human liberty.

Yet the unhappy effects of *this* form of concentration of power are spread out before our eyes for all to see. About 10,000,000 of us are unemployed and destitute. Hundreds of thousands have lost their homes and wander this country like tramps with no place to go. Farm tenantry has increased, and in the cities young men go about begging for the right to earn an honest living. For the first time in American history we have heard serious talk about *classes* instead of individuals. Our national debt towers over us, and our capital lies idle in the banks. And as a kind of explanation for this (but really as an excuse) we are told that the country has reached the limits of its growth and that the future has less to offer than the past. This, we are told, is the reason why power has been taken from us and placed in the hands of a few planners (whom we have not elected) in Washington. The increase in government power has thus been rationalized into a whole philoso-

Wide World Photo.

Convention Scene—Battling for New York Standard

Meeting the Delegations from Maine and Alabama

phy. It is a philosophy of defeat. We do not believe in it at all, yet its presence in government offices must be accepted as profoundly significant. For it indicates that the men to whom we have surrendered our power have *acquired a vested interest in depression.*

Now in seeking a solution to this problem it is necessary to avoid looking backward at what the Republicans did, or backward at what the Democrats have done more recently. We, the people, know that the solutions to the future do not lie in the past, whether remote or recent, except in a very limited sense. What we need is a new outlook, a new way of getting at things. Some of the recent reforms must be modified in order to protect our power; other, new reforms may have to be introduced. For instance, there has grown up a new concept of public welfare. Our new outlook must include this. Government, either state or federal, must be responsible not only for the destitute and the unemployed, but for elementary guarantees of public health, the rehabilitation of farmers, rebuilding of the soil, preservation of the national forests, clearance and elimination of city slums, and so forth. The need for these public works is not unique in this country. Warfare aside, it has been felt and answered by every civilized government in the world today, and some governments have gone much further than the New Deal, without disrupting their economies and without a philosophy of defeat. We, too, must be able to do that. We need also a new kind of budget, a new concept of the government's responsibility toward the taxpayers. We need a new foreign policy. In short, we must redesign a governmental system that, in view of our progress in other fields, has become obsolete. We do not want a New Deal any more. We want a New World.

And by what policy shall we be able to get this? Obviously such a policy cannot be stated in a word. A man would be something less than candid were he to claim to be able to spread it out all at once on the table, like a plan of battle. It is precisely because this cannot be done that we, the people, distrust political platforms. Yet it is also necessary, in the interests of candor, to lay down the fundamental principles and indicate the main objectives. This, at any rate, is all that is intended for the present "foundation."

THE BUSINESS HATERS

President Roosevelt's speech of acceptance at Chicago on July 2, 1932, was so encouraging to free enterprise that the New York *Times* had a five-column headline on the first page stating: "Roosevelt puts economic recovery first." Other newspapers interpreted the speech in the same way. But the awakening was swift and rude.

What happened was simply this. A great business depression had swept the country. We, the people, felt that businessmen had been chiefly responsible for the onset and violence of this depression. Maybe we were right: in any case we were disgusted with businessmen. We insisted on reforms. We insisted that certain guarantees should be established making it impossible for men to repeat in the future the abuses of the immediate past. And the Administration in Washington followed our wishes by instituting many (though not yet all) of the necessary reforms. But while this was going on something else was happening that we did not clearly perceive. Under the banners of "reform" there came to Washington, and there rose to power in various offices of the federal government, men whose hatred for business and businessmen surpassed the bounds of reason and good judgment. Business was set apart as a villain who had to be relentlessly harried. And government was promoted as a hero who could do no wrong.

Now this effort to separate "business" from the ordinary life of the people and to set it in a distinct and inferior category represents a profoundly false conception of our economic system. There are about 10,000,000 private enterprises in the U. S., which employ about 34,000,000 people, who in turn support many millions of other people. Business is a part of life and a way of life. By it we earn our bread, build our homes, care for our children, find expression for ourselves. Every one of us lives directly or indirectly by business — even the unemployed, whose funds come from the earnings of other workers. Obviously there are many things still wrong about business. Obviously when any one business gets too much power, that is a bad thing. But if we are to live, if we are to maintain our present standard of living, and, most of all, if we are to hope for greater things in the future, business must flourish. No single reform instituted by the New Deal, or for that matter no handful of reforms, would keep American business down. But the *attitude*, the intangible hostility toward this most fundamental part of our economic system has made it impossible any longer to act in a free and enterprising manner. And in spite of all the fine things that the New Deal has said about little business, little businessmen know that this anti-business attitude has hit them even harder than it has hit the big businessmen.

Indeed, to carry this point a step further, it is *business*, in the broadest sense of the word — including industry and technology, and including the modern farm, which is a business enterprise — that has made the American people so great. We are illustrious for our political system; we are becoming so in the arts; but our business acumen and our industrial might have never been equaled, and they remain the envy and wonder of the world. There is no need here to enumerate achievements that are familiar to all of us. The point is that these achievements were brought about by the application of certain principles — business principles. There have been bad business principles. But there have also been good ones; and every businessman knows that the good ones "work best" in the long run. These would include: strict accountability to profit and loss, measurement of risk and of the desirability of investment, clear and honest accounting, careful depreciation and building up of reserves, the enterprising use of assets, the development of markets, a respect for business ethics, and honor in the written or spoken word. Perhaps all of these principles can be summed up under the general head of common sense.

Now the American people have had administrations — chiefly Republican — that have encouraged the practice of these principles by private enterprise. But they have never had an administration of either party that has to any considerable extent *practiced* them itself. Since the government is not a business enterprise, this is quite natural: it could not, for instance, go in for "the development of markets" for itself. Yet there is a fundamental attitude that the government could, and should, adopt, if it were interested in building a New World. The government in that New World would have to have a sense of responsibility for the people's money: and this means more than just not stealing it. The government, as such, is a nonprofit enterprise, and in this country it must always remain so. But it is the biggest enterprise of any kind in the land. With vast sums of our money passing through its hands it has an inviolable obligation to see to it that *we, the people,* profit by that passage. If the government, besides providing the "ordinary" services of the departments, is also going to spend our money on enormous public works — which is certainly our wish — it must see to it that we get our money back, and something more besides. The government itself need not profit, but we must profit. So long as the government fails to accomplish this it is delinquent in its elementary business responsibility. And it is bound to prolong the depression. The losses it creates, whether through inefficient taxes, or through unnecessary interferences, or just by throwing money around in an unbusinesslike manner, must be absorbed by whatever profits we are making from our own enterprises. And this in turn means that we operate at less profit, or none at all; that the profit system *seems* to be failing; that national income does not rise; and consequently that wealth does not increase.

Now this is exactly what has happened under the present Administration. The primary criticism of the New Deal is not the size of its spending. This might be much curtailed; but we ourselves wanted it to be big, and even after economies it will remain big. But with its bias against business, the New Deal has not shouldered the elementary business responsibility that lies on government today. It has *lost* our money by the billion.

Before proceeding further let us examine this general point in more detail.

TAXES

We have heard a great deal about taxes from all sides. Businessmen tell us that the tax system has borne down so heavily on private enterprise that it has retarded the investment of new capital and the taking of risks. Various tax experts, on the other hand, have pointed out that we, the people, are much more highly taxed than we know. Our taxes are concealed. The average income in the U. S. is $480 a year and the average per capita tax, including federal, state, and local, is about $107.50 a year. And only a relatively small proportion of this can be shifted to "the rich" by any conceivable device. But even though our taxes are high, they do not seem to be high enough, since our government has run into debt for nine years in a row and has piled up the national debt almost to its legal limit of $45,000,000,000.

The complaint of business against the tax system arose originally from the anti-business attitude of the Administration already mentioned. After the New Deal had been in office a while the idea became to "soak business" — deliberately and maliciously. We, the people, liked that for a while, but it now appears to be a costly policy. Last year the Administration, sensing our attitude, made some modifications in the capital-gains tax. But these modifications have not gone for enough. A *businesslike* approach to the tax problem would involve an entirely different attitude.

First of all, such an approach would recognize that our enterprises are hurt, not so much from the size as the kind of taxes. British taxes were higher than ours (per capita) even before the war, but they were so wisely levied that economic conditions in Great Britain were improving. In most respects Britain was better off in 1938 than she had been in 1929, whereas we have never approached the 1929 level. Second, from a businesslike standpoint the aim of a government should be to raise its money as cheaply as possible.

Taxes may be expensive in two ways: they cost money to collect and they act as a brake on the economy. A businesslike administration would try to eliminate some of the present duplications in the collecting of our taxes; but, most of all, it would try to take the brakes off.

The cheapest tax is the inheritance tax, because to tax a man after his death does not affect his incentives so much as when you tax him while he is alive. On the other hand, a tax on profits is bound to be expensive because profits provide the incentive for a man to use his money and keep people at work — or even put new people to work. It is fair that the rich should pay proportionately much more than the poor. But it is foolhardy to deprive the rich of incentives for investing their money in ways that create employment, in new industries, and thus raise the people's purchasing power. Today our government levies terrific taxes on successful venture capital, whereas timid money, which buys government bonds and takes no chances, is hardly taxed at all. This is certainly a very expensive way to raise money. In various ways a businesslike government would learn how to tax timid money much more highly, while lifting part of the burden from venture capital; which would tend to encourage growth, put more people to work, increase the national income, and thus increase the total tax yield. While charging the same, the government would in that event get more. And this is a sound business principle.

SPENDING

In the ten fiscal years beginning in 1930, the federal government has spent a total of $66,000,000,000. Originally, the government recorded much of this enormous expenditure as of an *emergency* nature, and we approved it as such. Now we find that the word "emergency" has been dropped and that federal officials tend to think of the government as being engaged primarily in "spend-lend" programs. The President's last budget message is strikingly silent on any reference to "emergency," but refers instead to "the deliberate use of government funds and government credit to energize private enterprise." This is the theory that the government has to take charge of the economic revival because the people's industries are incapable of doing so. It leads to the theory that once recovery is achieved, the government must continue to sustain it. It means, finally, the transformation of our system of free economic enterprise into the totalitarian state.

It is necessary for us to get some simple things straight about this spending idea. In the first place, there is nothing whatever new about it. Our government has always "spent," in the sense of taking our wealth or credit and giving it back to us. It began by giving away our land to the settlers, or charging only nominal sums for it. It gave away our land to the railroads to subsidize them across our continent. It has spent our money in helping the ships and the airplanes, and in building billions of dollars' worth of roads. Our government has always had a spending program. And it always will.

But it will be observed, concerning those earlier spending programs, that they were shrewdly calculated *to help us to make a profit*. The money spent on roads, for example, has returned to us many times over, because it helped the automobile industry to grow, and with it the rubber industry and the oil industry and a hundred and one other industries in which millions of us earn our living. Spending need not be harmful to our system. It may be, and in the past has been, of enormous benefit to every one of us.

But in the past the government was never foolish enough to suppose that just spending, for the sake of spending, could accomplish anything. And indeed it has not. Ten years of spending, on a far more lavish scale than ever before, have failed to crack the depression. Last summer Congress refused to give the President the $3,000,000,000 he wanted for his spend-lend program, and he predicted that this action would retard industrial recovery. But his prediction proved to be inaccurate. There was an immediate *improvement* in business after the curtailment of government spending — even before the current war provided a temporary and artificial stimulus.

Spending is an economic problem. And the trouble today arises from the fact that our government has sought to solve it by social judgments. The social judgments are important. In many matters it is necessary to put them first. Yet they must be controlled in high office by a businesslike attitude. A businesslike administration would not go in for a public welfare project without making some careful and far-reaching measurements. It would have to consider each spending project — except those of a genuinely emergency nature — in the light of an *investment* for us, the people. The government will not always be able to find such good investments as the roads have turned out to be and sometimes, in the very nature of its trust, the returns on its investments must be intangible returns — as in the case of hospitals, for example. Yet good economic investments can be found. Slum clearance, for instance, should be carried much further than it has been. Slum clearance raises the standard of living of the families involved. It therefore raises property values and helps business in the surrounding areas. Another kind of investment might be research laboratories (somewhat like that at Langley Field) that small businessmen could use to help them compete against big business. Another might be the training of skilled mechanics. The point is that the choice of a businesslike administration would be highly selective. It would not be made *primarily* for the sake of spending some money, but *primarily* for the sake of generating opportunities for private enterprise. The fiscal policy would be subordinated to an economic policy.

THE BUDGET

Just as the accounts of a business provide the businessman with necessary controls, so a modern and efficient budgetary system would help a businesslike government to control its policies.

Our present national budget is like the little man on the stair — it isn't really there at all. We have never had a budget in this country — at least not as we, the people, understand the word. A budget, when you and I make it up, is, first, an estimate of what we expect to earn; and second, based upon that, an estimate of what we shall be able to spend. The government does not figure it that way. The government first determines what it would like to spend, then it considers how it is going to raise the money. Then it approves these calculations and calls it a "budget." But then it largely disregards the "budget" anyway and adds new expenditures to the existing ones. In the fiscal year 1934, for example, the amount of money *added* to the budget actually exceeded the original amount as specified. The "budget" specified $3,975,000,000, and the government later appropriated about $5,000,000,000 more.

If you ran down to Washington and asked to see the budget today, you would be shown a large book of several hundred printed pages. This is made up chiefly of a series of requests for money. These requests are written in that lavish spirit for which the government is famous and in almost complete disregard of financial rules that must be observed by business enterprises. Worse, unless you are an expert—and even, in some cases, *if* you are an expert—you will find it impossible to unscramble many of these expenditures and arrange them in definite categories so as to tell exactly what your government is doing. A businessman is held strictly accountable to his stockholders for money he spends for "expansion," "depreciation," "depletion," "welfare," "shop safety," "research," etc. No matter how complicated the business may be, no matter how many subsidiaries may be involved, it is always possible to tell the stockholders how much money is being spent, for what—and why. Thus, if it appears that a business is "expanding" too rapidly, or that there is too big an investment in handsome buildings that don't bring any immediate return, the stockholders' representatives can protest. But the present U.S. budget offers the people no such opportunity because it does not place the government expenditures on a rational basis.

Worse still, the government is not honest concerning some of the sources from which it gets money. It is one of the greatest holding companies in the world, owning and operating many subsidiaries, such as TVA, the Farm Credit Administration, the Reconstruction Finance Corporation, the Home Owners' Loan Corporation, the Federal Deposit Insurance Corporation, etc. These subsidiaries may sell their securities to the public and turn over the cash to the government. Such transactions would be outside the regular budget. The government could get this money and spend it—and does so—without saying anything about it in the budget.

The situation is so bad that a former regional administrator of the New York office of the Securities and Exchange Commission has roundly censured it. "The SEC," he says, "requires issuers of securities for public subscription to make a full disclosure of all material facts, and, where financial data are used, to present them on principles of sound accounting. The federal budget and balance sheet of federal investments as they are now set up fail clearly to meet the standards of honest disclosure, set by the federal government's own agency [the SEC]. Certainly no corporate borrower of funds from the public could get by on such shaky data as the federal government puts forth."

In earlier times it may not have been necessary for the government to manage a budget on a strictly businesslike basis. But today the need for public works, already outlined, makes it absolutely essential that it do a businesslike job. We, the stockholders, must know, for instance, how much of the government expenditure is for investment (such as low-cost housing) with a prospect of at least some financial return; and how much is for "investment" in projects like parks and health programs, from which no monetary return is to be expected. Above all, when the government actually gets into business, as with the TVA, it must set up reasonable valuations, just as the private utilities do; and it must show profits or losses based on these valuations. It may well be that we shall want to maintain a government enterprise at a loss, as we have maintained the Post Office on a subsidy basis for some hundred and fifty years. But if we are to have control over our fiscal policy we must know how big that loss is. In the case of the Post Office we don't.

Finally, until our government approaches the problem of the budget in a more businesslike fashion, there seems to be little realistic hope of balancing it. Here, we think, it is important to remember that in the beginning the budget deficit was not the fault of either party. Our government began to operate on a deficit in the year 1931, under a Republican administration. No administration of whatever character, even if it were composed entirely of angels, could have avoided a deficit in that year or the years immediately ensuing.

But today we cannot accept the position of some of the Republicans who demand an immediate budget balance, any more than we can accept the position of some of the ardent New Dealers who contemplate permanent deficit spending. We, the people, stand between these two extreme positions. We know that it is impossible to balance the budget this year. But we know, also, that just as no individual can exist for long on a policy of spending more than he earns, so no nation can live on such a policy.

And we say that any businessman, confronted with our situation, would work out a long-term plan for balancing his budget that would enable him to meet his obligations and get himself out of the red. First, he would economize as much as possible on his current operations. This would not get him out of the red because, as already pointed out, it would be necessary for him to undertake expensive public works or investments. So his second step would be to find out how much these public works amount to and what sort of a profit or loss to expect from them. He could then reduce or increase them according to some rational plan. Finally, he would make provision — no matter how hard or how slow it might be — to pay back the debt that he had incurred for these public works. Of course, in bad times, when his income was small and his expenditures necessarily high, these repayments on his debt might be little more than bookkeeping operations. Yet by them he would signify to the world that he intended to pay back, and not go on increasing his debt to infinity. And when times improved, he would demonstrate his good faith by actually shrinking his debt. A budget like that, based upon the most advanced business principles, has been in operation in Sweden for several years. And there is no reason why the U. S. should not have one.

So the first characteristic of a people's platform — a platform built for all the people, for national prosperity — must be a *businesslike* approach to the major economic problems of the day: to taxation, to public works, and to the national budget. This is just plain common sense. On the one hand, it would restore business confidence and get our wheels moving again. On the other, it would speed up social progress and reform. We all know that an enterprise in bad shape cannot do much for its workers — cannot raise wages or shorten hours or do any of the little things that make work pleasanter but that cost money. These things can be done only by a prosperous concern. And similarly the social progress that we have been trying to get for

Wide World Photo.

En Route to Speakers' Stand in Convention Hall

Thanking the Convention

the past eight years cannot really be achieved until our economy is put on a good business basis.

Finally, a businesslike approach, which would reveal to us where our taxes are coming from and exactly how our money is being spent, would restore to us full power over the fiscal affairs of our government: a power that we have virtually lost because our taxes are largely concealed and the plan of our expenditures is nonexistent. Thus our government's attitude has a direct bearing on that larger question, already mentioned, of our power. And it is time now to turn to this.

USURPATION OF POWER

When this country was founded our forefathers were extremely jealous of the people's power; they didn't want anybody to get too much of it. First, there were certain powers they didn't want to give to anybody at all, and these they incorporated in the Bill of Rights, guaranteeing free speech, a free press, free religious worship, protection of private property, etc. Then they said that the federal government should have only such powers as were specifically given to it; all others were left to the states. They went even further than that. Having given specific powers to the federal government, they divided these up into three parts: a legislature, an executive, and a judiciary. Thus the power of the federal government, besides being limited, was checked by a system of balances designed to prevent anyone from accumulating too much power in his own hands. No other country in the world has made so great an effort to protect its citizens from the exercise of arbitrary political power. Even in the great constitutional monarchy of England, a majority in the House of Commons can at any time eliminate freedom of the press or freedom of religious worship. Congress could not do that here — not constitutionally.

But under the guise of reform our government has broken through these limitations in several important respects. Here again we must be careful how we fix blame. Thus, in recent years, the federal government has supplanted the states, especially in its handling of the relief problem. The mayors of our great cities, indeed, do not turn for help to their state capitals so frequently as they turn to Washington. But this trend is not entirely the New Deal's fault. It has been encouraged by the states themselves, and by us, the people.

But the time has now come to reassert the principles of a limited federal government, because if this trend is not stopped the people will lose the powers that the Constitution gave them. They will lose them to an all-powerful central government. Too much power has already been lost, for instance, in the decisions of the *new* Supreme Court. Everyone supposed that Mr. Roosevelt lost the Supreme Court fight, but in the end he accomplished his objective, because, by the death or retirement of five judges, he has been able to appoint new men. This new Court has already rendered a number of decisions vastly increasing the power of the central government at the expense of the citizen. In former days the people could protect their enterprises by resort to the courts. Today the highest court in the land cannot be relied on for that purpose.

But the most flagrant and ambitious extension of government power has come through the so-called executive commissions like the SEC, the FCC, the CAA, etc. These bodies concentrate literally immeasurable power in the hands of a few men *whom we, the people, did not elect.* These men are today making the rules for the enterprises of the American people, large and small. There is no assurance that these rules will apply even for a reasonable time; they may be changed from day to day. When the rules are broken, these same commissioners prosecute the offenders and decide the penalties. Thus the American system, once so carefully protected and balanced, has given way to a system in which a few men make the laws for industry, prosecute the violators of the laws, and sit as judges over the violations.

James Madison, who was chiefly responsible for the Constitution of the U. S., stated: "The accumulation of all powers — legislative, executive, and judiciary — in the same hand . . . may be justly pronounced the very definition of tyranny." And Lord Bryce said: "The separation of these powers is the fundamental characteristic of the American National Government and upon it depends the freedom of the individual." In a recent decision, the Federal Circuit Court of Appeals in Chicago reversed a ruling of the National Labor Relations Board against a corporation. In doing so it criticized the conduct of the board's examiner as being "hostile" to the company concerned. The report stated: "This record, as a whole, discloses the danger of imposing on a single agency the multiple duties of prosecutor, judge, jury, and executioner." The effect of granting such powers to individual men has been to put government on a *personal* basis. The personal good will of commissioners is of extreme importance to American businessmen. Of course, as a result of this, no businessman dares to criticize a commissioner, because he knows that if he does so his company will suffer for it. This is not theory. It has actually happened to many businessmen — most of whom, however, do not dare even to talk about it. No such undemocratic fear exists toward, let us say, the judges of a state supreme court; for judges do not make their decisions on personal grounds of like and dislike or upon economic differences, but upon the law.

We, the people, know that it is bad government to make decisions upon any other grounds. It is not representative government as we conceive it, or as it was conceived by our forefathers. It is government depending upon the caprice and favor of a few men. And as such, it is government under which American industry cannot operate with assurance and confidence. There are, of course, dozens of illustrations of wise and fair decisions made by these federal commissions. We have sufficient confidence in our fellow men to believe that the majority of those in federal office try to carry

216

The Convention Greets Its Nominee and His Wife

Meeting Reporters and Campaign Workers Next Morning

out their duty honestly. But that is not the point. The point is that our form of government was designed to prevent the assumption by a few men of such enormous power over our lives and industries. Excessive power in the hands of big corporations is an evil. But it is no more evil than excessive power in the hands of big government. As we are opposed to industrial monopoly, so are we opposed to government monopoly. The American principle excludes these enormous concentrations. We, the people, wish to keep the control to ourselves.

And so to our first demand, that the government's approach to our economic problems be businesslike, we add this second demand that, through the law, the power be returned to us that we rightfully possess. And as a matter of fact these two propositions are inseparably linked. A man running our government with a businesslike point of view, as steward of the people's prosperity, would not permit his representatives to jeopardize prosperity by intimidating businessmen on a personal basis. Nor, on the other hand, could he afford to allow any business to become too powerful. This is because an undue concentration of wealth and power threatens the welfare of the little businessman. Yet it is upon the little businessman — including in that term the American farmer, who, let none forget, is *in business* — that a shrewd administrator of government affairs would most rely, because the little businessman provides the economic system with a broad, competitive base. The technological and financial encouragement of the little businessman is bound to result in a more intensive development of new inventions and new enterprises than is the encouragement (as at present) of economic concentration in big corporations. A man dedicated to getting the most for the people out of their money in a spending program, for instance, would do things that would help the little businessman to *compete* against the big one. In this way he would get manufactured prices down without legislation. And lower manufactured prices mean a higher real income for us, the people.

FOREIGN POLICY: WAR

We conceive that if these fundamental principles are applied to our domestic problem they will enable *us* to build that New World that we all desire. For the point is that *we* must build it — not government. Yet today the whole world is so closely knit, the oceans are so small, and the peoples of the world are so dependent upon each other, that it is not realistic to make domestic policies without considering their relationship to foreign affairs. Of all the major powers, the U. S. is the least dependent on others. We are most amply endowed with resources, we have the highest standard of living, and we have the greatest geographical protection. Nevertheless, we are not entirely isolated. It makes a great deal of difference to us — politically, economically, and emotionally — what kind of world exists beyond our shores. We cannot build our New World here without taking that other world into account.

The international situation, of course, is complicated at present by war. If it were not for the war — or wars — it would be easier to lay down a long-term policy that would have constructive results. As it is, the best we can do is to use elementary common sense. This, it seems, is just what our political leaders refuse to do. Some political leaders, both Democratic and Republican, have taken extreme positions to which common sense cannot possibly follow them.

Let us take the case of Finland as an illustration. Technically, Finland is not yet a belligerent — it never declared war on anybody and never started any fighting — so that it does not come within the provisions of the Neutrality Act. Finland has also paid the interest on its debt to the U. S., so that it does not come within the provisions of the Johnson Act. So it was proposed in Congress that the government should grant a loan or credit to that country.

But it was just at this point that the isolationists in Congress assumed a position that a contortionist might have been proud of. It was well known that Finland was in desperate need of airplanes and munitions generally, and wanted to use the money to buy those things from the U. S. and other countries. The isolationists, however, said that Finland should be permitted to use this money only for nonmilitary purposes. And the reason given for such a restriction was that the sale of military equipment might lead us into war. It

221

might be regarded as a hostile act by Finland's enemy or enemies.

Now we have been sure for a great number of years that we don't want to have any part in anybody's war. We have had some wars of our own in the past. We now think we have outgrown them. If we and our neighbors on this hemisphere are left to ourselves, we can get along very nicely without any military activity. And we don't think that we should be called upon to settle the boundaries of a less fortunate continent. Also, we have a vague feeling that if the situation were reversed, if the hostilities were over here, we should not see any country in Europe coming over to stand beside us on the battle line.

Nevertheless, we have very strong sympathies in the war between Finland and the U.S.S.R. We feel that there can be no question as to which is right and which is wrong. We know that if Finland is able to keep the U.S.S.R. at bay, then world peace and economic order are a little more assured, whereas if the U.S.S.R. sweeps over Finland, then world peace and economic order are in greater jeopardy. In short, we should like to help Finland so long as we can do so without getting into war.

And, clearly, we have a right to lend, buy, sell, or borrow, with respect to any country we designate. We might well drop that right for the sake of peace. Yet we must remember that no foreign nation wants to have the U. S. as its enemy or will contrive to find a cause for hostility with this country. In fact, its tendency will be the other way — to overlook annoyances in the hope of keeping us neutral. If the aggressive countries today — the U.S.S.R., Germany, and Japan — were looking for quarrels to pick with the U. S., they could find plenty of excuses. The government, for instance, has encouraged the sale of military equipment to England and France. It has also expressed its vigorous opposition to certain of the policies of Germany, the U.S.S.R., and Japan. It has even gone so far as to call for a "moral embargo" against Japan. It has refused to recognize the state of Manchukuo, which the Japanese took from China, and it has similarly refused to recognize Germany's conquest of Czechoslovakia or the conquest of Poland. It has withdrawn our Ambassador from Germany. The President of our country has written notes of protest to the dictator of Germany and the dictator of the U.S.S.R., etc. No one of those things involved us in a war, and neither will a loan to Finland, however the Finns use the money.

It does not seem to us that our foreign policy need be complicated by the obsessions of the extremists on either side. Our political foreign experts should get rid of the habit of whispering through the window and slipping things down the back alley. Our foreign policies should be forthright and clear. We are opposed to war. But we do not intend to relinquish our right to sell whatever we want to those defending themselves from aggression. And we are not so foolish as to believe that these sales of products at our ports, with our ships withdrawn from combat areas, can possibly involve us in hostilities.

But underlying the immediate issues arising out of the war there is a deeper need. We, the people, want to know where we are being led. We want some reasonable and effective standard by which we can measure our foreign policy, year after year. And this standard, to be realistic, must be harmonious with our domestic policy. Just as it is necessary to put our own house in order on a businesslike basis, so it will be necessary, in the long run, to develop a businesslike foreign policy. The aim of such a policy would be, on the one hand, to protect our interests against the encroachment of others; but, on the other hand, to further our interests, increase our markets, and put our capital to work by helping other countries to make a profit too. This is a sound business principle. But hitherto it has been obscured in our foreign policy by emotionalism and domestic politics.

Take the problem of the Hull trade agreements, for example. Here again there has been a tendency for the Democrats to huddle in one corner shouting their enthusiasm, and the Republicans to huddle in another, prophesying calamity. We, the people, had better confer by ourselves.

One of the things that made this country great was the fact that it represented the greatest free-trade area in the world: its citizens have been able to ship their products for several thousand miles, up and down and crosswise, without trade restrictions or tariff barriers. If Europe had been like this, the history of the world would make pleasanter reading. Of course, in view of the discrepancy in standards of living, this sort of free trade cannot be world-wide. Yet the importance of trade to us is incalculable. Before the depression our foreign trade totaled in the neighborhood of $9,000,000,-000 a year; at the bottom of the depression it had shrunk to $3,000,000,000 a year. We thus lost a $6,000,-000,000 business, and rather more than half of it represented a decline in our exports. Obviously, if we could get that market back today it would mean a lot to the man who is looking for a job, or the farmer who is looking for a buyer. But while our foreign trade has recovered to about $5,000,000,000, further recovery is closed because all the great trading nations of the world, including our own, have set up tariff walls to keep out each other's products.

Now obviously it will not do for one great nation to become a free-trade country by itself. For the U. S. to erase its tariffs all at once would be ruinous to our people and many of our industries. The present Secretary of State, Cordell Hull, who is a wise and temperate man, realizes this. And so he adopted the *reciprocal* trade agreements as a step toward increasing our foreign business gradually. Under this policy the U. S. takes up the problem of tariffs with each country separately; lists the products that it would like to export; studies a similar list submitted by the other country; and then a deal is arranged, each country making such concessions as it can, with the least possible harm and the most possible benefit to its own people. This agreement is then extended to apply to other countries too. What could be simpler or more in accord with common sense? What could be better qualified to benefit us, the people *as a whole?* Of course we have to make sacrifices. But the point is that, owing to the way the agreements are negotiated, the sacrifices are always, and should always be, less than the benefits gained. That is, we, the people, profit.

We do not put much faith in the figures cited by the Republicans to show how damaging these Hull agreements have been, or in the figures cited by the Democrats to show how profitable they have been. It may be years before conclusive results can be shown. But it is inconceivable to us that prosperity can be reestablished without any foreign trade. And it seems clear that if we are to have foreign trade it must be done on a reciprocal basis. We, the most successful people in the world at business and industry, know that there are two parties to every trade, and that one cannot always profit at the expense of the other. It is of vital importance to us that the other party profit too.

And this leads to a final point regarding our foreign policy. From an international point of view our outstanding characteristic is our high standard of living. We wish to preserve this. But the bigger the difference between our standard of living and that of other nations, the more difficult our foreign relations are bound to be. Low-standard-of-living countries are not able to buy from us, nor do we want to endanger our own

Meeting the Press the Morning After

Relaxing at New York Theater After the Convention

standard of living by admitting their goods (in competition with our own) produced at coolie wages. On the other hand, high-standard-of-living countries, like England and Canada, have in the past provided the best markets for our goods. It seems clear to us that the best foreign policy for the U.S. is one that will, in the long run, *help to raise the standard of living of the rest of the world.*

Admittedly, this is a very elastic criterion. Yet it does provide a policy by which to shape our relations with other countries. Since war in the long run destroys the standard of living, we will not cooperate with—we are against—any aggressor nation. On the other hand, since the democratic system has done more than any other political form to raise the standard of living of the people who have adopted it, we wish to cooperate with and assist genuinely democratic countries. As time goes on, and as peace is restored, this policy might be applied to our sister republics in this hemisphere, and our sister democracies elsewhere, with some considerable effect. Our gold, our financial reserves, our trade, can all be instrumental in building up the standard of living of other peoples who, like us, seek peace, progress, and plenty.

———————

A month later, Russell W. Davenport, managing editor of *Fortune Magazine*, resigned his position to give all his efforts "to furthering the nomination of Wendell L. Willkie as Republican candidate for President of the United States." Mr. Willkie had not yet announced his candidacy, but he had said that it was an honor that he would not refuse. He told Davenport, "I am greatly interested in convincing the public of certain principles of government which I believe very deeply." Finally, affairs came to the pass that Mr. Willkie felt it necessary to make a public decision and announce himself as a candidate for the nomination, and Mr. Davenport became his official manager. Mr. Willkie insisted, however, that there must be no effort to raise a great campaign fund. He would make no attempt to gain delegates by promising Federal positions of any kind or by making inconsistent statements to please sectional groups. In other words, he would take the nomination only if he were left free, without commitments which would tie his hands in the campaign—or afterwards. After the convention, he made the statement that the total expense of the central organization that promoted his candidacy was less than $25,000 and that his own expenses were less than $4,000, which he paid himself.

Root claims to have mailed 600 Willkie-for-President petitions last April, each containing space for fifteen signatures. By the 19th of June, 275,000 copies of the petition had been sent out; and 100,000 more had been ordered. Willkie clubs sprang up all over the country until there were over 500 of them grouped into the Associated Willkie Clubs. Root organized the Willkie Mailing Committee. Men and women volunteered in large numbers to help send out literature, make up lists, interview callers, arrange for Willkie Clubs throughout the country, or do any of the other things necessary to carry on the campaign. Davenport had the task of inter-

viewing important personages in various places and seeing that they were aware of the rising tide in favor of
Willkie.

The text of one of the Willkie petitions follows:

WILLKIE FOR PRESIDENT

We, the undersigned people of the United States,
citizens of Indiana, believe that Wendell Willkie
should be elected President of the United States.

After twenty years of post-war government, both
Republican and Democratic, there are about 10,-
000,000 of us Americans who are unemployed and
destitute. Hundreds of thousands have lost their
homes and wander this country with no place to
go. Farm tenantry has increased, and in the cities
young men go about begging for the right to earn
a living. For the first time in American history we
have heard serious talk about CLASSES instead
of individuals. Our national debt towers over us,
and our capital lies idle in the banks. As a kind
of explanation of this we are told that the country
has reached the limits of its growth and that the
future has less to offer than the past. This, we
are told, is why power has been taken from us and
placed in the hands of a few planners (whom we
have not elected) in Washington. This is a philosophy of defeat.

Because Wendell Willkie does not believe in this
philosophy of defeat we welcome him. We call for
his election as President because he has a proven

belief in free enterprise, yet he can contemplate with equanimity the great changes in society which these moving times require; because he knows that business is a part of life and a way of life, and that only through BUSINESS-LIKE government can there be social profit for the people; because he has a hatred of persecution inherited from his ancestors who fled to these shores to escape the persecutions of their era; because alike on matters of taxation, foreign affairs, human welfare and the other cardinal issues of the day he has displayed an insight, a candor and an absence of vindictiveness which are unique in the political theatre of our time.

But more than all else we know that Wendell Willkie will not let us down. He will not let us down because he understands some fundamental things about us. He knows that we believe in personal integrity—and he shares that belief. He knows that we have a deep and abiding faith in our country—and he shares that faith. He knows that NATIONAL prosperity is more beneficial to us than sectional or occupational prosperity. He will be the defender of our power, and not of the power of any institution or favored group. What Wendell Willkie believes he has written and spoken without quibble. But the essence of his political philosophy is in his heart, as it is in the hearts of us the people of the United States.

International News Photo.

Reading Telegrams at Home After the Convention

Giving Autograph After Conference at Statehouse, Des Moines, Iowa

Below this petition was space for the names and addresses of signers and instructions to send the signatures to a Wilkie-for-President Club. "The purpose of this declaration," read a note, "is to dramatize the strength of the people's demand for Willkie."

From the local clubs went out postcards with a message like this:

Dear ....

Will you risk a few cents to make Wendell Willkie President? If so please . . .

1st—Send copies of this message to five of your friends.

2nd.—Send a card to "The Willkie for President Club" Elwood, Ind. saying, "I'm for Willkie for President" and sign your name and address.

                        Sincerely,

P.S. If you want to know about Willkie, ask the "Willkie for President Club" for a copy of *"We, The People"*.

The Elwood club sent out postcards to every state in the Union boosting Willkie's nomination, and replies came from almost every state.

In the meantime, Mr. Willkie himself was filling numerous speaking engagements and expressing his views in the public press. From early years, he had been concerned with freedom. Before the Toledo Civic Forum and Rotary Club, he gave the following address, which is reprinted here from *World Digest* for August, 1940:

OUR GOVERNMENT IS A DICTATORSHIP
Wendell L. Willkie

If I had the time, I should like to write a history of mankind's long struggle for freedom. It would begin back in the shadowy reaches of the cave when men first banded in groups to achieve a certain measure of freedom from the perils of the jungle. It would tell of the wars of subject races to escape from a foreign yoke; or the revolt of a people to overthrow the despots which they had themselves created. It would discuss the methods whereby, in time of peace, men have sought to protect themselves against the exercise of arbitrary power, whether in the hands of the government, the Army, business, or the Church.

When I was a young man in college, this nation was engaged in a great liberal crusade. Its leaders were three great Americans—all three very different in personality and background—Theodore Roosevelt, Robert LaFollette and Woodrow Wilson. Its objective was to free the American people from the excessive power of Big Business.

American business corporations did not really get started until after the Civil War. It was not until the latter part of the 19th century that the manufacturing corporation began to flourish. This country was growing fast. Its basic industries, led by the railroads, were rapidly being organized into gigantic industrial combines, which sought to suppress all new competitors. The Sherman Anti-Trust Act in 1890 was not able to stem this mounting tide of economic power. The corporate monopolies began to extend their influence to the State Legislatures and even to Federal authorities. By the first years of this century they threatened to overshadow the people's government itself.

Then the liberals rose in alarm and began their long and colorful campaign to restrain this corporate power. The oil trust, the tobacco trust, the beef trust and other monopolies were dissolved. The railroads discontinued the issuance of political passes. What Wilson called the "money trust" was destroyed by the Federal Reserve Act of 1913. So successful was the campaign, that, in his message to Congress in 1914, Woodrow Wilson felt able to state:

"Our program of legislation with respect to business is now virtually complete. . . . The road at last lies clear and firm before business."

Perhaps the restraints thus imposed upon corporate power would have been effective if it had not been for the World War. But wars are not good for freedom. They destroy the essential balance of society.

In the inflation and false prosperity following the World War, business men, drunk with power, and a public, drunk with money, broke down the safeguards protecting individual liberties. When Sir James Bryce, the great critic of our civilization, wrote his concluding chapter of "The American Commonwealth" in 1920, he pointed out that "the growth of vast fortunes has helped to create a political problem," and warned us against "the irresponsible nature of a power which three or four men, or perhaps one man, can exercise through a great corporation." Rightly he prophesied that this would be an outstanding problem in those next few years.

In the money-mad period of the Twenties the heads of some of our corporations forgot their primary function—that of running a business enterprise in a way that would be sound for the worker, the consumer and the investor. Instead of attending to the duties of management they began playing with corporate structures as with a child's building-blocks, becoming promoters rather than business men. And some financiers in Wall Street and elsewhere, instead of serving as a link between the savings of the people and the enormous capital needs of industry, became jugglers of finance, concerned primarily neither with the investor nor the investment, but with making money and securing power for themselves.

In the normal course of events we should have corrected that condition, but the depression overturned this corporate tyranny almost overnight.

For a while I hoped that the New Deal would replace it with a truly liberal faith. But the leaders seemed to be motivated not by love, but by hate; they preferred to punish rather than to reform; they wanted to destroy the evildoers, even if the doers of good should also succumb. The purpose of this new government was not to eliminate monopolistic control, *but merely to change its ownership.* Today it is not Big Business that we have to fear. It is Big Government. The abuses that corrupted the 1920's have been transferred from Wall Street to Washington.

Four abuses were charged against business in the Twenties. The first was the concentration of excessive power in the hands of a few men; second, the use of this power and the money that went with it to influence political decisions; third, the manipulation of financial markets to the detriment of the investor and the enrichment of the manipulator; fourth, the ruthless determination to destroy opposition and create a monopoly.

Every one of those abuses exists today. We can repeat each one of those accusations. But the responsible party today is not the nation's business, but the nation's government.

For example, on the first point, never before has this country experienced so extraordinary a concentration of power in the hands of a few men as in the government today. All of the safeguards erected by the American people against too autocratic a government have been invaded. The powers once reserved to the States have been largely transferred to the Federal Government. And the Federal courts, which have the responsibility for protecting the rights of these States or the rights of individuals against Federal legislation, have been largely staffed by appointees of the new system.

For a time the Supreme Court stood in the way of this political usurpation of power. But today, laws regulating national activities or national industries must cover so many different and complicated conditions that Congress cannot do anything more than prescribe the basic

239

principles; it must turn over to a commission the duty of formulating the rules.

It would be obviously impossible, for example, for Congress to write a law governing labor conditions which would be applicable, without further interpretation, to every business or occupation, large or small, anywhere in the country. Such a law can only be written in general terms; it must set up a commission to make it effective and to adjust it to different situations. So the commission, in effect, writes the law. The commission also prosecutes those who violate it. Then, having acted as both legislator and prosecutor, the commission undergoes another lightning change and becomes a judge sitting in judgment on its own case.

In the main, these commissioners are not appointed by Congress. They are not elected by the people. They are appointed by the Executive and responsible to him alone. Thus the people have no control over these individuals who write, enforce and judge the rules for the 10,000,000 business enterprises of America.

Sometimes such a government has been honestly administered, sometimes dishonestly. But it is not the kind of government to be tolerated by an upright and independent people.

This concentration of political power in the hands of a few men not controlled by the people is just as bad as the concentration of economic power in the Twenties; and it leads just as readily to the second abuse of which business was accused a decade ago: namely, the use of this power to influence political decisions.

Today there are thirty-one government agencies which can lend money and there are dozens of government commissions regulating industry. Cooperation between the two offers frightening possibilities. A couple of weeks ago the chairman of the National Labor Relations Board testified that the Board had an arrangement with the Reconstruction Finance Corporation whereby that corporation would withhold any loans to companies which the Labor Relations Board had on its blacklist!

Personally, I think that various government officials have made considerable effort to prevent the use of relief funds to influence the voters in political campaigns. Yet, we know that relief funds have been used in that way, just as they always will be where there is too much irresponsible political power. The influence of the purse is a great and grave influence, and a government which distributes billions of dollars on spend-lend programs holds a terrifying weapon over the heads of those who displease it.

And this brings us to the third abuse once lodged against business and now lodged against government: namely, the manipulation of the financial markets.

Not even a totalitarian state has more financial powers than those exercised by the present Administration. Such "rigging" of the markets as the bankers were able to achieve in their hey-day in this country was as nothing compared with the financial puppet show put on by the government, in which, by pulling this string and that, the government can lower or raise

241

interest rates, security prices, purchasing power and values.

For example, in 1934, in order to raise prices, the government decided to lessen the value of the dollar and increase the price of gold; so, since that time the government has been buying all the gold offered to it and paying a price of $35 an ounce. No other country and no other individual will pay such a price. If the United States should withdraw its offer, the price would immediately fall. As it is, the United States is slowly accumulating all the gold in the world. In these days gold is dug up in South Africa only to be promptly buried in Kentucky.

The government also maintains a stabilization fund of 2 billion dollars. The operations of this fund are kept secret by the Treasury. All that is known is that the Treasury uses these funds from day to day to buy and sell foreign exchange in order to keep the ratio at the level which it deems to be satisfactory.

The government also influences interest rates and security markets through the activities of the Federal Reserve Board. There was a time when this Board was independent of the government. Today, however, it is dominated by the United States Treasury. By open market activities through the Federal Reserve banks interest rates, credit conditions and security prices generally are subject to the influence of the government.

These specific powers over money, over credit, over securities, over prices, etc., are perhaps of less importance than the government's general spending policy.

242

When the government first started on its enormous expenditures for relief and public works, there was no question about their necessity. As emergency measures —and that was how they were regarded—they were sound and desirable. Unfortunately, because government rarely relinquishes a power which it has once obtained, the emergency character of these measures was shortly disregarded: the government embarked upon vast continuing spend-lend programs designed not to promote private enterprise but to promote direct financial and economic activity by the government.

But even the "spend-lend" phrase was found somewhat unsatisfactory. It was too tentative and temporary. Shortly the government began to talk about *permanent government investment*.

The fourth charge which the liberals hurled against the corporation presidents and bankers in the Twenties was that they created monopolies designed to eliminate all opposition. It is a curious feature of human nature that as a man's power increases, so does his sensitivity to opposition. We are familiar with the phenomenon of the dictator who rages at the slightest reflection upon his motives or his methods. Messrs. Stalin, Hitler and Mussolini are notorious for their dislike for anyone of a skeptical nature; even the minor voices of opposition disturb them. The same weakness can be detected in many members of the present government. Public rebukes from the highest sources have been given to newspaper reporters who have become critical of Administration policies. A chairman of one

of the most important Federal commissions has long
followed the practice of writing to, or calling upon,
those newspaper correspondents or editors who have
seen fit to criticize the chairman's actions. Pressure
upon the press is a favorite weapon by which the Administration seeks to silence the opposition—and to the
credit of the press, it is generally a futile one.

You will remember that business fiercely resented
the efforts made by the liberals to restrain the excessive powers of business. Big Business did not want to
be checked in its control over the lives of the people.
Now that the pendulum has swung the other way, we
find that government has the same attitude. It does not
want to be checked either. Just as business fought
against regulation, so government today resists every
effort to curb its authority.

Too much power in the hands of a few men; use of
money to influence political decisions; manipulation of
the markets; destruction of all opposition—these were
the charges hurled against the economic monopolies of
the first quarter of this century. They are the charges
which we make today against the present form of government. The banners used by the true liberals today
are the same banners used by the liberals in that other
time. They bear the same inscription; they make the
same appeal; but the citadel of corporate power against
which they once were led has fallen. It is a new citadel
of entrenched political power toward which they must
be directed.

The people of the United States will begin their real recovery from the depression when they demand that a curb should be placed upon a government grown too great. In the past ten years there was only one major activity in this country which has shown any real expansion: that is the United States Government. Government employment has increased nearly 100%; government borrowing has increased over 150%; government expenditures have increased nearly 200%, now amounting to over nine billion dollars. The government has created dozens of commissions and spent millions on buildings to house them. It has enormously added to its powers over our lives, and it has largely delegated those powers to Federal commissioners who are not responsible to the people nor to the Congress, but are appointed by the Executive.

The purpose of government is not to increase its own powers, but the powers of the people. The purpose of government is to make men free. In his book, THE NEW FREEDOM, Woodrow Wilson made this memorable statement:

"The only thing that can ever make a free country is to keep a free and hopeful heart under every jacket in it. Honest American industry has always thriven, when it has thriven at all, on freedom; it has never thriven on monopoly. It is a great deal better to shift for ourselves than to be taken care of by a great combination of capital. I, for my part, do not want to be taken care of. I would rather starve a free man than be fed a mere thing at the caprice of those who are organiz-

245

ing American industry as they please to organize it. I know, and every man in his heart knows, that the only way to enrich America is to make it possible for any man who has the brains to get into the game."

Woodrow Wilson was talking about economic monopoly, but his statement is just as true when it is applied to political monopoly. If the Government of the United States will sincerely dedicate itself to the purpose of making men free to carry on their economic enterprises, and of making it possible for "the man with brains to get into the game," then this country, with its great trade area, its natural resources and its business genius, will resume an economic progress which will be even greater in the future than in the past.

———

At Manhattan Center, New York, a Hoosier Box Supper was held May 21. Main Street of Elwood, Indiana, was set up in the center. The school bell from the red brick school building was the signal for the lap supper served in boxes, such as were used at the old-time box suppers. At the "school exercises," prominent Hoosiers from New York and Indiana recalled Willkie's schoolboy days and other interesting events in his career. The event of the evening was an address by Mr. Willkie.

From the beginning, there have been objections to Mr. Willkie as the presidential nominee of the Republican Party. Strict party men, of course, have objection to him on the ground that he has been a Republican only a short time. He was a member of the Democratic Jackson Club at the university and has been

246

a Democrat for many years. He voted for Franklin D. Roosevelt for president eight years ago and contributed $150 to the campaign fund in that year. This, he says, is the expenditure he most regrets.

At first he was in hearty agreement with the New Deal. In fact, he is not now opposed to the ends which the New Deal set out to accomplish. Writing in the *New Republic*, he maintains that there should be no sacrifice of the moral gains of recent years, that we must have "truth in securities," that we must have "social security" for the aged and the unemployed, that we must have suitable provisions for collective bargaining. When asked recently why he left the Democratic Party, he replied, "The Democratic Party left me."

That is why, four years ago, he voted for Landon and why he is today a Republican. It is only the amateur debater who thinks that he must deny everything his opponent says. Experience proves to him that often his opponent has part of the truth and that, by denying that portion of truth, he cuts away the ground under his own argument. Consequently, he finds that, by accepting the good in his opponents' argument, he strengthens his own. This is something difficult for the politician to understand; he feels that he must condemn his opponent completely and that any admission that there is something to be said on his side is weakness.

Mr. Willkie believes that the political reformer is not the only one who wants to see high wages, security for the helpless, honest markets, and industrial peace. These are also the hope and aim of intelligent businessmen. He does believe, however, that to gain these ends by the surrender of that priceless heritage of America, freedom, is to throw away the baby with the washwater.

The common purpose of all liberals, he maintains, is to make men free. This freedom is not divisible. One can not have industrial freedom where there is not freedom of speech and freedom of religion. One can not have political freedom without industrial freedom.

He maintains that the government has been visiting upon all American industry the sins of a few corporations. He says that government hostility has broken down in large measure the old American faith that has built our nation. He does not believe that the true liberal desires to punish those who see matters differently but fights only for causes which will benefit both his opponents and himself. He has expressed himself so definitely on the problems of today that there need be no doubt where he stands. He maintains that the New Deal has attempted to substitute government by persons for government by law, government by fear and prejudice for government upon principles. Since the Democratic Party had left the ideals for which he thought it should stand, he could no longer be a Democrat. He believes that the country should come first and party afterwards. Party partisanship, he believes, is nonsense, and the important thing is what one believes. He refuses to denounce all the acts of the Democrats or praise all the policies of his own party.

Nevertheless, those who had worked for years in the Republican Party felt some resentment against the newcomer. Besides, they doubted his ability to get votes;

but, when petitions began to come in by the million, this doubt melted.

Another objection was that he seemed disinclined to work for the nomination. However, after he had definitely announced that he was a candidate for the nomination, this ground for objection vanished.

The campaign for Willkie's nomination grew. The Willkie Clubs exchanged ideas, and a new plan in one club was quickly adopted by all. Reprints of *We, the People* were circulated. Petitions and letters poured in on the delegates. So time fled to the opening of the National Republican Convention in Convention Hall at Philadelphia at eleven o'clock in the morning, June 24, 1940.

The interest and excitement of that convention can be compared only to that at the Republican Convention in Chicago May 16, 1860. Then, too, the country had problems which had aroused great feeling. The man from Illinois seemed to have little chance. It was expected that Seward would receive a two-third vote from the 428 delegates on the first ballot; but, as the organization was perfected and the platform was adopted, it became apparent that there was a definite drift from Seward. On the first ballot, Seward received 173½ votes, Lincoln 102. On the second ballot, Lincoln received 113 votes; and, on the third ballot, he received a majority. Feeling ran high, not only then but during the ensuing campaign.

One thing soon became evident at the convention hall at Philadelphia—this was an unbossed convention. There was no powerful politician telling the delegates how to vote. The seasoned politicians agreed that there was no chance for Mr. Willkie. However, millions of petitions were pouring in on the delegate—for Willkie. No one knows just how many had signed the Willkie petitions, but it has been estimated that there were signatures of between four and five million voters. At first, there was a tendency to believe that these were not genuine; but checks tended to indicate that they were. Telegrams overflowed the desks of the delegates—for Willkie. From Elwood alone, 516 voters sent the following telegram to the Indiana delegation: "WE UNDERSIGNED CITIZENS OF ELWOOD, INDIANA, HAVE SUPREME CONFIDENCE IN THE ABILITIES OF WENDELL L. WILLKIE, OUR FELLOW TOWNSMAN. EACH OF US HAS SHARED THE EXPENSE OF THIS TELEGRAM THAT WE, AS INDIVIDUALS, MAY RESPECT- FULLY SOLICIT YOUR SUPPORT FOR WENDELL FOR PRESIDENT OF THE UNITED STATES."

Letters and postcards cluttered the delegates' quarters— for Willkie. From Elwood, Indiana, alone came to the Indiana delegation more than 3,000 letters and 800 cards asking them to vote for Willkie. The gallery was designed to seat 17,000; but it is estimated that there were 26,000 there—for Willkie.

The 22nd National Republican convention was called to order by National Chairman John Hamilton. The resolutions committee made its report. At ten that night, Harold Stassen, Governor of Minnesota, made the keynote speech of the convention. The Credential Committee labored all night. The next morning, Representative Joseph W. Martin, of Massachusetts, was elected permanent chairman of the Convention. Ex-

Register News Bureau.

Discussing American Defense with George A. Wilson, Governor of Iowa

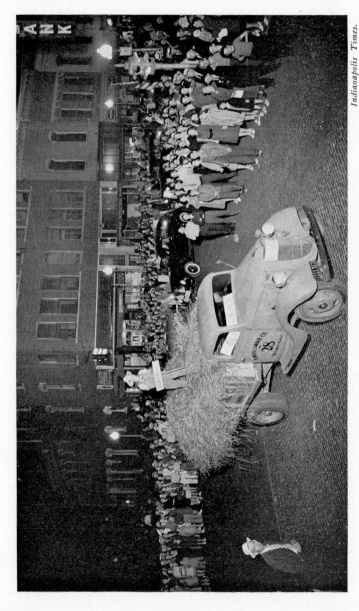

Elwood Greets "Farmer Willkie" in Celebration of His Nomination

Indianapolis Times.

President Hoover made an address the following night. Wednesday, the platform was adopted.

Meanwhile, the candidates and the delegates had been busy. Campaign headquarters had been set up by the managers and the candidates. Senator Taft had set up 102 rooms for his quarters; Attorney Dewey's headquarters comprised 78 rooms; Mr. Gannett's headquarters consisted of 48 rooms in addition to the Harvard Club; Willkie's headquarters consisted of a two-room suite in the Benjamin Franklin Hotel, and he had no manager. It became noised about that Willkie was the man to stop, and the candidates and delegates busied themselves in a "Stop Willkie" campaign.

On Wednesday, the party platform was adopted. Came four-thirty in the afternoon, and the time for nominations.

John Lord O'Brian nominated Dewey, and the New York delegation swept down the aisles. Other standards joined the procession—Illinois, Oklahoma, Kentucky, Florida, Idaho, Wisconsin, South Carolina, Montana, and Tennessee. Joseph W. Martin, Jr., of Massachusetts, minority floor leader in the House of Representatives, chairman of the convention, was unable to restore order for twenty-five minutes. Then came the seconding speeches by Lester H. Clee, Newark, New Jersey; William E. King, Chicago, Illinois; Albert J. O'Melia, Rhinelander, Wisconsin; and Mrs. M. E. Norris, Burlington, Washington.

Gannett, Rochester publisher, was nominated by Representative James F. Wadsworth of New York and received a two-minute ovation.

Taft was next put in nomination by Grove Patterson, editor of the Toledo *Blade*. The Ohio delegation led the twenty-minute demonstration which greeted his name. In the parade up and down the aisles were delegates from Indiana, Kentucky, California, Texas, Utah, Iowa, Washington, Arkansas, Colorado, and Georgia.

Then Representative Charles Halleck of Indiana got the floor. At the mention of Willkie's name in the second paragraph of his eleven-page speech, he was interrupted by a loud roar of applause. When shortly afterwards, Halleck said that Willkie could keep us out of war, there was a loud chorus of boos, which were drowned out by shouts of "We want Willkie." The rest of the speech was punctuated by alternating and intermingling boos and cheers. At last the speech was over—twenty minutes past ten.

There was a pause while one could take a good breath. Then the noise began. The parade started. There was an attempt to steal the New York banner, and a fight started. The Rhode Island banner wavered and then joined the slow parade through the crowded aisles. There was a fight about the Virginia banner. The organ stopped playing as a signal for the cheers to stop, but to no avail. A dozen states had joined the parade. At thirty-six after ten, Chairman Martin made himself heard to the effect that the seconding speeches were yet to be made and that it was getting late. "We want Willkie!" greeted his announcement; but, at ten-forty, order had been established. The explosion of the convention had occurred, and the delegates knew that "We Want Willkie".

The nomination was seconded by Representative Bruce Barton, of New York; Governor Ralph Carr, of Colorado; Miss Ann Stuart, of Saint Paul; and Governor Raymond E. Baldwin, of Connecticut. (The original penciled speech by Governor Baldwin is now in the archives of the State of Connecticut, but a photostatic copy is in the library of Indiana University.) Then the convention adjourned until the next morning, when the remaining nominations were made. Thirteen candidates were in the field.

At four-thirty Thursday afternoon, Chairman Martin called the convention to order; and preparations were made for the roll call of the states in alphabetical order.

It was not till Arkansas was called that the first votes were given Willkie—two votes. California cast one vote more than it was entitled to, and a roll call was demanded. The clerk on the New Hampshire delegation gave seven votes for Bridges and one for New Hampshire (which was changed to a vote for Hoover). At every Willkie vote, the gallery cheered. While the vote was being tabulated, the gallery chanted "We want Willkie." The result of the first ballot was Dewey, 360; Taft, 189; Willkie, 105; Vandenburg, 76. The other votes were scattered among the other nine candidates.

The second ballot began at 6:06. California added two more to the Willkie vote, to the noisy approval of the gallery. Maine gave the first big break with nine votes. Then came seven from Massachusetts; seven from Missouri. So it went on, a nibble here and a nibble there. When the clerk read the result of the second ballot, Dewey had 338, a loss of 22; Taft 203, a gain of 14; Willkie 171, a gain of 66; Vandenberg 73, a loss of 3; James 66, a loss of 8.

It was time for a recess. Deals of all kinds were discussed. Telephone calls, hurried meetings, whispered conversations! Everywhere, the question was: Could Willkie be stopped?

The recess ended at 8:30, and the third ballot began. Arizona added six to Willkie's slate. Delaware was solid for Willkie. New York changed 14 votes to the Willkie column. There were signs of cracks everywhere in the two leading organizations. Dewey had lost 23 votes; Taft had gained 9; Willkie had gained 88 in that one-hour ballot.

The fourth ballot got under way. Minor changes here and there went almost unnoticed. Illinois reserved her vote to the end, and then announced that her block of Dewey votes had dwindled from 47 to 17 and threw the bulk of her vote to Taft. Taft, the audience believed, was on the way. But wait, the announcement of the results was a surprise—Dewey 251, a loss of 64; Taft 254, a gain of 42; Willkie 306, a gain of 47. Willkie was ahead! One of the delegates led the gallery in the chant "We want Willkie."

In the fifth ballot, Florida changed its majority from Dewey to Willkie; Kansas gave her solid vote to Willkie; New Jersey gave 26 of its 32 votes to Willkie. Oklahoma gave Taft her solid vote, asked for a roll call count, gave Willkie 4. These were the signs. The clerk read the result: Willkie had 429 votes; he needed but 72 to win.

It was now 12:20—Friday morning. A motion to adjourn was refused by the chairman. One more ballot! Dewey's vote had dwindled to 57. Maine, which had been solidly for Willkie, passed. Vandenberg released his delegates, and Willkie got 35 of the 38. New Jersey, Oregon increased Willkie's lead. Pennsylvania passed. By one o'clock Willkie was within 2 votes of nomination. A minute later, Pennsylvania cast its total of 72 votes for Willkie. Governor Bricker of Ohio moved to make the vote unanimous but was ruled out of order. At 1:40, everyone was ready to make the vote unanimous. It is unanimous. Willkie isn't coming, the word is passed along. The band and organ play "*Off to Work We Go*", the tune to which Philadelphia workingmen had been marching singing a parody favoring Willkie. Willkie was the Republican candidate for the presidency of the United States.

What had Willkie been doing during the convention? A very unconventional thing. He had kept open house. There was no red tape about seeing him. He was ready to answer any question put to him about his political views—a "dangerous" practice, many politicians think. He had held conference with Landon, with Hoover, with Hamilton. He had been himself, and he had won delegates.

During the convention, millions of American citizens had been listening to the reports over the radio. When the voting began, business in Elwood hit a new low, for everyone was standing about the radio listening or watching the bulletins at the office of the daily. As the Willkie vote mounted, the excitement in Elwood mounted

257

with it. When it became evident that Willkie was to be nominated, people left their houses and drove about the streets, honking their horns and shouting for Willkie. The sidewalks, usually deserted at one o'clock in the morning, were alive with people. Wendell Willkie of Elwood was about to become the Republican candidate for the presidency of the United States!

During the balloting, Mr. Willkie had remained in his headquarters. As success seemed more and more certain, reporters had hurried from Convention Hall to his suite to join the crowd already there. When the result was assured, the crowd called upon Mr. Willkie for a speech. Mounting a chair, he told them that this was just the beginning of the fight, that he intended to do everything he could to bring about American prosperity, build an adequate defense, and restore national unity.

The delegates and the visitors were hoping that he would come to the hall, and word to that effect began to spread. Finally, he sent a message to Chairman Martin, who read it and announced, "He wants me to thank you for your loyalty and generosity. He is grateful that this has come in a free convention where there has been deliberation such as no party has had before." Congratulations came to the convention from Mr. Hoover. The latter, Mr. Dewey, and Mr. Taft, among many others, sent him their congratulations.

Mrs. Willkie had been in the gallery. When his vote had passed the required number, she had hurried home to her hotel. Calling her husband, she asked if she had to come to his quarters. Upon being assured that she did not, she asked him to hurry home. Disheveled, wet with sweat, tired, he left his suite for home. Police and friends had to hold back the great crowd that wanted to shake hands and speak to him.

When the convention reconvened on Friday afternoon, there remained but the problem of choosing the running mate for Mr. Willkie. It was known that the minority Senate leader, Charles L. McNary, of Oregon, was Mr. Willkie's choice; but it was not known if he would accept. Representative Dewey Short, of Missouri, and Senator Styles Bridges, of New Hampshire, were presented. When Senator McNary telephoned from Washington that he did not desire the office but that, "like a good soldier," he would accept if his name were presented, he, too, was nominated. He was approved by a vote of 890 to 110 for the other candidates. On Representative Short's motion, the vote was made unanimous.

Soon, the report spread that Willkie was coming. He arrived in the midst of a hard shower, paused a little while in the anteroom with Mrs. Willkie, and then entered the hall preceded by a captain of police. At once the cheering began. Torn paper fluttered down on them as they made their way down the aisle, Mr. Willkie smiling and waving to the crowd, responding to hurried handshakes from those along the way.

Chairman Martin introduced "The charming lady who will be the next mistress of the White House." She was vociferously cheered. Then the chairman presented the man who "meets the demand for a leader who can seriously tackle these great problems which now confront

259

America." Showers of confetti rained down on them. At last, there came a calm; and Mr. Willkie addressed the delegates and visitors:

"I doubt if in the history of American political conventions any convention has ever been presided over with more impartiality, more fairness, and more ability than this one has been presided over by Joe Martin.

"I want to say to the members of this convention that as your nominee I stand before you without a single pledge, promise, or understanding of any kind except for the advancement of your cause and the preservation of American democracy.

"It is a moving and appealing and almost overwhelming thing to be the nominee of a great free convention of this kind.

"I doubt if any man who has not experienced it could imagine and understand the full import of the emotion it brings to one when such obligations come to him.

"I wanted to come here to you this afternoon, not to discuss policies or principles, but merely to thank you, to express my appreciation, and to tell you of the deep sense of dedication I feel to the cause that you have asked me to lead.

"Democracy and our way of life is facing the most crucial test it has ever faced in all its long history; and we here are not Republicans, alone, but Americans, to dedicate ourselves to the democratic way of life in the United States because here stands the last firm, untouched foothold of freedom in all the world.

"And as your nominee I expect to conduct a crusading, aggressive, fighting campaign to bring unity to America, to bring the unity of labor and capital, agriculture and manufacturer, farmer and worker, and all classes to this great cause of the preservation of freedom.

"I think as one who has been a member of each of those classes in the course of my brief life, I understand that in America we all have a common purpose at this time that this way of life shall not pass from this earth. For the rehabilitation of American economy; for the building of an adequate defense so that no dictator, however strong, may seek to strike; for the unity of our people; for calling again America to its great tradition of progress, I pledge myself to you; and I ask each of you to join with me in this great crusade.

"Forty-eight days ago, and only 48 days ago, I started out to preach to the American people the doctrine of unity, the doctrine of the destiny of America; and the fact that I am the nominee of this convention at this time proves conclusively how appealing is this simple doctrine to the American people.

"So, you Republicans, I call upon you to join me, help me. The cause is great. We must win. We cannot fail if we stand together in our united fight. I thank you.

"Now I am going to sleep for a week!"

Among the many telegrams pouring in on him was one from the Madison County Republican Central Committee asking him to make his acceptance speech at Elwood. When the first booster meeting for Willkie was held in the Elwood gymnasium, before his campaign for nomination was well started, he had talked to the crowd by telephone from New York and had told them that, if he were nominated, he would make his acceptance speech from the steps of the old high school building at Elwood. He had not forgotten that promise and repeated it now.

For a week, he had had four hours or less of sleep a night and had promised Mrs. Willkie that, win or lose, he would take a few days' rest. First, however, was the necessity of meeting the friends who had helped him in his last-minute campaign. It was necessary, also, to meet the new Republican National Committee, including the thirty new members, and to select a national party chairman. He held late conference with Governor Harold E. Stassen, of Minnesota, his convention floor leader; Governor Raymond E. Baldwin, of Connecticut; Representative Charles Halleck, of Indiana; Samuel F. Pryor, Connecticut national committeeman; and Representative Martin, chairman of the convention. He announced that he would resign as president of the Commonwealth & Southern Corporation and from his other business affiliations and devote his whole time to the Republican campaign. The national committee appointed a sub-committee to confer with him later about the appointment of the national party chairman.

At last, he could get away. With his wife and son, he sailed the yacht *Jamaroy*, the guest of Roy W. Howard, of the Scripps-Howard newspapers, for a week-end rest. On Monday, he resigned his position with the Commonwealth & Southern Corporation and made preparations to resign from his other business affiliations.

When questioned by reporters, he said that he hoped President Roosevelt would be his opponent—a hope realized by the Democratic Convention on July 18. When asked why, he replied, "Because I'd love to beat him. Not that I think he would be the easiest man to beat, but he's the author and the ablest advocate of the New Deal, and the people have a right to hear from him." When told that the White House would be closed until September 1 to be redecorated, he remarked, "I think that is a very courteous thing to do for your successor."

The next evening, Mr. Willkie told his family that he would like to go to a theater and "just relax," although he had not been to a theater all winter. He assured them that nobody would notice them; but, when they entered, the audience stood up and cheered. When the lights went off, the crowd shouted, "We want Willkie." At the intermission, he was besieged with handshakers and autograph-seekers.

July 2. Willkie announced that he would accept small campaign contributions but none for over $5,000. "The more one-dollar and five-dollar ones, the better," he said. He would make no appointments to the diplomatic corps nor to public offices in the United States in payment for contributions. He said that he intended to enforce the provisions of the amendment to the Hatch Act fixing $5,000 as the maximum gift by any individual to a political party and limiting the total expenditures of any political party in any one year to $3,000,000, whether Congress passed it or not. All contributions of ten dollars or more would have to be checks or other forms so that they could be matters of record. He criticized the custom of soliciting subscriptions under the guise of advertising in campaign booklets, etc., and said that this would not be permitted. He stated that he had made no pledges, direct nor indirect, about appointments or official acts in case he should be elected.

After consulting Martin and other prominent republicans, he announced an advisory committee to co-operate with him and the National Committee. Besides Chairman Stassen and Halleck, those on the committee are Representative Joseph W. Martin, Massachusetts, Republican leader of the House; Representative William Ditter, Pennsylvania, chairman of the Republican congressional committee; Senator John Townsend, Delaware, chairman of the senatorial campaign committee; Davis S. Ingalls, Cleveland, Ohio, preconvention Taft manager; Ruth Hanna McCormick Simms, New Mexico, preconvention Dewey manager; Governors Raymond Baldwin, Connecticut, and Ralph Carr, Colorado, who seconded his nomination; Oren Root, Jr., New York volunteer organizer of the first Willkie club; Mrs. Ruth DeYoung Kohler, Wisconsin, once a Chicago newspaperwoman; and Paul Krusi, chairman of the Tennessee delegation to the Philadelphia convention. The National Republican Club of New York City, although he was not present, accepted him as a member.

July 3. Willkie received many letters from Democrats pledging him their support. He stated that the chief issue in the campaign is the New Deal philosophy of government, which is that of increasing the power of the state over the individual. Before he became a candidate, he called attention in the *Atlantic* to the over eighty departments, bureaus, and commissions carrying on the work of the government. Although their members and directors have not been elected by the people, they have so much discretionary power that all business, large and small alike, are in confusion because of the ever-changing rules, which take the place of laws passed by Congress. The present Supreme Court, too, he said, had encouraged a "vast, ineffectual, and expensive" centralized government.

He promised to make an intensive campaign covering the entire country. In his organization for the campaign, he was trying to secure complete Republican unity, as he hoped to secure national unity in case of election.

July 4. Part of the day was spent preparing for a meeting with the subcommittee to determine the national chairman and receiving political visitors. Mr. Willkie saw himself in the movie short "Information Please." He was wildly cheered as "our next president."

July 5. Mr. Willkie held a three-hour session with the advisory committee. Most of the fifteen members of the executive committee were selected, among them Mrs. Grace Reynolds, of Cambridge City, Indiana. Mr. Willkie announced that he would wait until the Democratic platform and candidate has been announced before preparing his acceptance speech. Representative

Halleck, of Indiana, and Representative Martin, of Massachusetts, called on him.

July 6. Willkie met again with the advisory committee. All but one member of the executive committee were decided upon. He also held conversations with Martin and Samuel W. Pryor, Jr., national committeeman from Connecticut. In an interview published in the Jewish daily *The Day*, he said, "I . . . clearly asserted my position against race hatred, bigotry and Hitlerism . . . long before I even thought of being a presidential candidate. I did it solely because I wanted to express my protest against all Fascistic persecution methods.

"If anti-Semitism should spread its roots in the United States as it has done in most of the countries of Europe, then it would definitely be a calamity for the United States."

July 7. Mr. Willkie wound up his affairs preparatory to leaving New York. He spent the day at his home greeting friends and meeting important Republicans.

July 8. Mr. Willkie flew to Washington, where he met Senator McNary. He outlined to him his campaign plans and his decision to make Representative Martin national chairman. The two nominees were the guests at a dinner given by the 169 Republican Representatives and the 23 Republican senators. Meeting newspaper men, he answered all questions except those relating to policy, saying those would be reserved until he made his acceptance speech. He promised to make a strong campaign in the South.

July 9. Willkie selected Joseph W. Martin, Jr., as chairman of the Republican National Committee and manager of his campaign. John D. Hamilton, who has held this position since 1936, will be executive director of the national committee. Martin will receive no salary; Hamilton will continue to receive $15,000 for salary and $10,000 for expenses. Russell Davenport, former managing editor of *Fortune Magazine*, will be Willkie's personal representative. Oren Root, Jr., will continue to organize independent clubs for Willkie. The full membership of the executive committee was announced. Willkie met Dewey for the first time. Dewey, Taft, and Vandenberg promised him their support. Mrs. Willkie arrived in Washington from New York. Mr. Willkie left on a plane for Colorado Springs, Colorado, with his wife, five books, and twenty newspapermen. The party stopped at Chicago, and he gave an interview over the radio. Here and at Omaha, he shook hands with many well-wishers and wrote autographs. He was greeted at Colorado Springs by a crowd chanting, "We want Willkie." Willkie asked Governor Carr, who had flown from Denver to meet him, if this was a paid gallery. When Governor Carr told him, "This is the voice of Colorado," the crowd yelled, "Yes."

July 10. Willkie conferred with Governor Carr. He took a short automobile ride through nearby mountains but spent most of the day in his apartment. He had luncheon and dinner with a number of prominent people.

July 11. The press reported that Willkie was "loafing" on this day. After an early morning swim, he drove through the mountains. He told the press conference that he had been reading the dissenting opinions of the late Justice Holmes. He received visitors from Elwood.

He announced that he intended to go directly to the people in this campaign and use the radio only as a secondary means of spreading his views. [For a number of years, there has been a growing tendency for people in high places to use ghost writers and to put together sections of speeches prepared by others. This makes it impossible to know the real views of the speaker. When Mr. Willkie was asked who was going to help him write his acceptance speech, he replied, characteristically, "I roll my own." This does not mean, of course, that he will not try to get information from those who may have it.] He announced that he would consult with numerous party leaders about various phases of his speech before beginning actually to draft it. He worked out vacation plans with Governor Carr. At his press conference, he told the reporters that the New Deal is seeking to deprive its opponents of their civil liberties. He cited the attempt to insert in the Hatch Bill (prohibiting political activities by state, county, or municipal employees paid in part by Federal funds; limiting campaign subscriptions to $5,000; and placing a $3,000,000 limit on the expenditures of a political party in any one year) an amendment prohibiting political activity by employees of privately owned utility firms.

July 12. Willkie was the guest of the Colorado Springs "community cowhands" at an open-air, informal dinner. On his way to Denver, he spoke impromptu at Littleton and Englewood, Colorado.

Willkie spoke on the steps of the Colorado state house to about 9,000 people in favor of an adequate naval defense. He addressed the Colorado State Central

Elwood High School Gymnasium Ready for Huge Willkie Rally

Indianapolis Star.

Indianapolis Star.

Elwood Boy Scouts Boost Willkie

Committee: "I dedicate myself to three things: One, a united people without class distinction or class hatred; two, rehabilitation of our national life; three, the building of an adequate defense program. I have no delusion that the rehabilitation of our economic life is not as important, or even more important, than a defense program. If we make our economic life vibrant and vital and have a united people, no dictator or totalitarian ruler will ever strike at this country." After the luncheon, he shooks hands with an estimated 6,000 people. He and Mrs. Willkie flew from Denver to Colorado Springs.

July 13. Willkie held a conference with Mrs. Ruth Hanna McCormick Simms; Wayland Brooks, Republican candidate for Illinois senator; and Richard J. Lyons, Illinois Republican leader. Willkie agreed with Brooks that the campaign would be fought out on the question whether the nation approved of centralizing "power over the lives of all the people in the hands of a few or whether we will maintain and develop an adequate, mechanized, motorized, armed defense and at the same time preserve our system of government, with a strong national economy sufficient to produce and maintain the necessary armed defense."

July 14. Willkie motored with Governor Carr to the Gunnison River to the annual fish fry, where fishermen caught 5,000 trout for the 10,000 guests. Fish and buffalo meat were cooked over open camp fires. He returned to Colorado Springs by plane.

July 15. Willkie listened to the opening of the Democratic Convention. Before the opening of the Republican Convention, he had predicted that it would nominate him on the sixth ballot; now he predicted that Roosevelt would be nominated on the first ballot by the Democrats. He intended to listen in to see if his forecast was correct. He went down from his apartment to greet a group of 362 tourist school teachers. He visited the ranch owned by the International Typographical Union and inspected the Holstein Friesian cattle there.

July 16. When asked to comment on Speaker Bankhead's keynote address at the Democratic Conventions, he agreed with Bankhead's condemnation of the speculative orgis of the Nineteenth Century and dictated this statement at his press conference:

> "I always have thought that such speculation was to be condemned, whether it was in the securities of utility companies, vending machine companies or took the form of gambling in foreign exchange, such as German marks. I am very proud that I had absolute-nothing to do with that phase of economic life.
>
> "I have spent a substantial part of my time during the past seven and one-half years protecting the investments of the people against the assaults of their own government."

He sent Herbert Hoover, by a press representative, an oral invitation to visit him in Colorado.

July 17. Taking a portable radio along to keep in touch with the Democratic Convention, Mr. Willkie attended an entertainment at the old gold mining town of Central City, Colorado. He had conferences with numerous visitors. He was watching the light opera *The Bartered Bride* in the opera house at Central City when he received word that Roosevelt had been renominated.

Speaking from a hotel balcony, he told the mining crowd that "War destroys the culture that you know and it can be maintained only in peace. I dedicate myself to the preservation of that peace."

July 18. Willkie conferred with Governor George A. Wilson, of Iowa, on the farm problem and asked him to arrange a conference of farm leaders in Des Moines. He lunched with Professor and Mrs. Paul Harmon, of Indiana University, formerly of Elwood. In the evening, he had a conference with the editor of the *Chicago Tribune*.

July 19. An increasing number of Democrats announced that they would bolt the Democratic party. Some announced that they would support Willkie. Willkie said while a luncheon guest at the Denver Union Stockyards:

"I shall make no pretense of noble motives. I am not going to tell you of my unselfish sacrifices in seeking to be president of the United States. I frankly sought the opportunity to run for president on the Republican ticket because I have some deep-seated convictions I want to present to the American people and which, if I am elected, I want to carry into execution.

"I know something about the democratic way of life, not from books or theorists, but from experience. I know the democratic way of life as an experience. . . . I learned about civil liberties, not in textbooks, but in the hard struggle for survival.

"I know your aspirations and your hopes. I know your resolve that this great democracy shall be preserved at all hazards. If you elect me president, you will have someone who understands the everyday problems of everyday people. I have lived them and glory in it."

He conferred informally with cattle and sheep men about the economics of cattle and sheep raising and the laws regulating grazing. They also discussed the sanitary regulations governing the importation of cattle from other countries and also the reciprocal trade agreements.

Mr. Willkie visited a beet-sugar factory; the Federal Veterans' Hospital; and an 80-acre beet, melon, and corn farm near Denver.

July 20. Among those whose views in regard to the agricultural situation Mr. Willkie is seeking to find was George N. Peek, former Agricultural Adjustment Administrator. A number of Democrats from all over the country, including Louisiana sugar planters, have sent Mr. Willkie word that they would support him for the presidency.

July 21. Mr. Willkie did some preliminary work on his acceptance address. He talked with Minneapolis publishers and other callers.

July 22. Mr. Willkie announced that his acceptance speech would be delivered in Elwood, Indiana, on August 17.

July 23. Mr. Willkie attended Cheyenne's Frontier Days Rodeo at Cheyenne, Wyoming. Enroute, he spoke from the platform of his car at Brighton, Colorado, and at Greely, Colorado. At Cheyenne, he said, "I know there are thousands of men qualified for my position, public or private. In this country, there is no such thing as the indispensable man. The very essence of democracy is that it develops initiative and the energies of men."

He announced that he wanted no paid speakers in his campaign. He believed that there would be no lack of people who cared enough for the principles for which he stood to carry on the campaign without pay. In the evening, he addressed a meeting of Wyoming Republicans.

July 24. Mr. and Mrs. Willkie visited the Church of Jesus Christ of Latter Day Saints and spoke with the president. He addressed the crowd at the pioneer celebration at the Salt Lake rodeo grounds. He had conferences with a number of party leaders and editors. Late in the afternoon, Mr. and Mrs. Willkie attended a reception in their honor. In the evening, they attended a rodeo at Ogden, Utah.

On their way back to Colorado Springs, he stopped at Denver to confer briefly with Representative Halleck in regard to plans for the acceptance ceremony at Elwood on August 17. Altogether, on this trip, Mr. Willkie traveled 1400 miles in fifty-six hours and made seven speeches.

July 25. In Colorado Springs, he consulted with Homer E. Capehart, in general charge of the acceptance ceremony plans, and with Arch N. Bobbitt, Republican state chairman of Indiana, in regard to the plans for August 17. A meeting to be held August 5 at Des

Moines to discuss agricultural questions with representatives of nine states was announced.

July 26. Willkie held conferences with prominent Republicans. He considered invitations to speak at various points in the South and spent some time working on his acceptance speech.

The advisability of setting up a new party as a means of allowing Democrats to vote for him without losing their party affiliation was considered. This might be called the Democratic Union Party or the Democratic Unity Party.

July 27. Willkie received—and had been receiving daily—assurances of support from many prominent Democrats. After a conference with a Republican group from Nebraska, he announced that he would see fewer visitors until his acceptance speech is prepared. The Republican National Committee announced the first scheduled campaign speech. This will be before the National Federation of Women's Republican Clubs on September 20 in Detroit, Michigan.

July 28. Willkie worked with secretaries, making rapid progress on his acceptance speech.

July 29. Willkie made a press statement that this was a crusade, rather than a campaign—a crusade for a return to basic American principles, a crusade which wipes out party lines. He received few visitors, spending most of his time on his acceptance speech. It is to be a declaration of principles and will treat questions of foreign policy, agriculture, labor, etc.

July 30. In reply to President Roosevelt's comments that deserting Democrats were actuated by love of dollars rather than love of humanity, Mr. Willkie called particular attention to the support of Al Smith, former governor of New York, and of Samuel Seabury, former associate justice of the Court of Appeals of New York and crusader against the Tammany machine. He called attention to Smith's charitable and philanthropic works and said: "He was a great liberal governor of New York. As a matter of fact, his liberal principles were those adopted by his two successors, Franklin Roosevelt and Governor Herbert H. Lehman. I am greatly gratified also that a man of the great public standing of Samuel Seabury—and the things for which he stands in the way of clean government in opposition to machine rule—should endorse me."

On a previous occasion, Mr. Willkie had severely criticized the corrupt political machines in a number of our large cities.

With the rough draft of his acceptance speech finished, Mr. Willkie began definite consideration of campaign plans. He announced that on August 3 he would hold a campaign organization conference in Colorado Springs. He talked with Russell Davenport, who is co-ordinating the work of the independent Willkie clubs.

[The deadline for the publication of this book requires the cessation of the story of Mr. Willkie's life at this point.]

Elwood Rally

Meanwhile, Elwood has been the scene of intense activity. After the spontaneous celebration the night of the nomination, a great mass meeting was scheduled for the night of July 2 in the high school gymnasium as a "tribute to Wendell."

The celebration, however, began early in the day. Flags and banners were displayed from homes and business houses. Boy Scouts, wearing high hats made from Willkie posters, met incoming motorists and wired posters on their bumpers.

When it grew dark, there was a torchlight parade with red fire and everything. Captain Nuzum, former chief of police and a warm friend of Willkie; Homer L. Chaillaux, of Indianapolis, Chairman of the National Americanization Committee of the American Legion; and William Sayer, of Indianapolis, Department Adjutant of the American Legion, led the parade in the first car. Frank Willkie, Wendell Willkie's uncle, and his wife; Michael J. Fogerty, Chief of Police; and Arthur E. Harrell, founder of the Willkie-for-President Club of Elwood, were in the second car. Former classmates of Willkie came next. The high school band and American Legion drum corps added life to the procession. The parade continued with almost every automobile in the city decorated with bunting, crepe paper, and Willkie-for-President signs.

One car was topped by a stuffed eagle. Trucks bore red and white banners reading "The Pride of Elwood," "Our Favorite Son," and "Win With Our Hometown Boy." On one truck was a load of hay, on which stood an overalled farmer labeled "Farmer Willkie." Large trucks from the canning factories lengthened the parade. The half-hour parade ended in the gymnasium.

Dr. R. R. Ploughe was master of ceremonies, and the Reverend Robert W. Sage, pastor of the First Baptist Church, gave the invocation. Dr. G. V. Newcomer, chairman of the Elwood Willkie-for-President Club made a short talk, after which a quartet from Indianapolis sang. Then Arthur E. Harrell, Secretary-Treasurer of the Willkie-for-President Club read a telegram from Mr. Willkie:

"I appreciate beyond words the many kind expressions which the people of Elwood have made prior to and since my nomination. As you perhaps know, I have announced that I expect to make my acceptance speech on the steps of the old high school building if that is satisfactory with school authorities. I hope at that time I have the great satisfaction of seeing many of you and thanking you personally."

The address of the evening to the 3,000 persons who packed the gymnasium and to the large crowds outside, for whom amplifiers had been erected, was made by Homer L. Chaillaux. He spoke of the dangers from demagogues and the necessity of using our best intelligence to understand our problems and to find solutions for them.

This was in no sense a political meeting; it was a token of respect for a fellow townsman who had brought honor to himself, and so to Elwood. There were visitors from Noblesville, Indianapolis, Tipton, Anderson, Alexandria, Marion, and Kokomo. Newspapermen from far and near were present to spread the news that Elwood rejoiced in the success of her own Wendell Willkie.

Soon after this, Lodge 368 Benevolent and Protective Order of Elks, of which Mr. Willkie had been a member while in Elwood, reinstated him and voted him a life membership. To this, Mr. Willkie responded with a cordial letter of acceptance.

Even if there had been any tendency for the people of Elwood to be indifferent to their famous fellow-townsman, the reporters, photographers, and curiosity-seekers would have made it impossible. Everyone who knew anything about the Willkies has been pumped by scores of inquirers. Every spot connected with their lives has been photographed innumerable times. Signs have been erected on the outskirts of the city announcing that Elwood was the "Home of Wendell Willkie." Signs have also been put up to mark the various homes of the Willkies, the school which Wendell attended, and other places of interest to sight-seers.

Before the date of the notification had definitely been set, John Stout, a 17-year-old boy of Handley, Texas, decided that he would not run the risk of missing it. With 300 Willkie buttons given him by the Texas-for-Willkie Club of Dallas to distribute on the way, he started out on his bicycle at 5:20 on July 8. He distributed his buttons and heard much approval of Willkie on the way. When he approached Elwood on July 22, he was surprised by a delegation of police and over a hundred townspeople who greeted him and escorted him into the city. He had come much faster than he expected; and his parents and brothers did not arrive in Elwood, by automobile, until the next day. They are visiting with relatives until after the notification ceremonies.

Most of all, however, the people of Elwood have been enthusiastic about the plans for the acceptance speech of their hero. At first, it was supposed that this event might take place as Mr. Willkie had planned, from the steps of the old high school building, those steps above which still stand out THE HOPE OF OUR COUNTRY. This, however, was found impractical as news began to come in that state and local delegations were coming with large groups to attend this event.

Soon after it was confirmed that Mr. Willkie would make his acceptance speech here, a group met to consider plans for that occasion. This group consisted of George M. Bonham, Mayor of Elwood; E. Wayne Drake; F. Van Tine; O. D. Hinshaw; Dr. G. Newcomer; Floyd Walker, of Lapel; and Ray V. Gibbens, Republican County Chairman. The problem at once assumed large proportions; and a number of subcommittees were formed —committees on housing, transportation, parking, publicity concessions and food, first aid, decorations, traffic, reception, information, amplification, press and radio, water and sanitation, and police escort for Mr. Willkie and other dignitaries. As it became more apparent that the attendance would be large, the State Republican Committee was notified; and the plan was submitted to it. On July 15, representatives of the State Republican Committee and of the National Republican Committee met with the local general committee. Homer E. Capehart was placed in charge as general director over all the committees.

281

Notification headquarters had been established at 1113 South Anderson Street. This home had been built by the American Tin Plate Mills as a home for its manager but was now vacant. Each room of this large home has been made into an office fully staffed for the enormous amount of detail work involved, for it now seems that there will be many more than a hundred thousand—some claim that there will be almost 300,000—visitors to Elwood to hear Mr. Willkie.

This, of course, makes it impractical to have the main address before the old high school building. All the plans are subject to change, as new information and new conditions come to the attention of the committees. At the end of July, however, rather definite plans have been made. On Friday, August 16, Mr. and Mrs. Willkie will go to Rushville and visit with Mrs. Willkie's mother, Mrs. Wilk. It is probable that Rushville will take this opportunity to show its enthusiasm for "Rushville's Son-in-Law." Saturday morning, August 17, Mr. and Mrs. Willkie will leave Rushville by special train accompanied by a large corps of newspapermen and photographers. They will remain in the car after their arrival here until 1:30, when he and the immediate members of his party will be called for by the reception committee.

The Indiana University Band and the Culver Black Horse Troop will act as his official escort and will conduct him to the entrance of the old high school building. There he will greet his former schoolmates, teachers, and old friends and make a short address. The parade will then move to Callaway Park, where the notification ceremonies and acceptance speech will be made, probably around three o'clock.

Bands will play throughout the day. There will also be a program by radio, movie, and stage stars to entertain the crowds waiting for this event.

Three hundred fifty acres north and east of the park have been contracted for by the Parking Committee to be used for parking automobiles, and two hundred more are available if needed. Fences will be removed, and everything done to simplify the parking problem. This will enable vast numbers to park within a fifteen-minute walk of the speakers' stand. One-way traffic will be enforced over most of the roads leading to this region. Two hundred state police will be assigned to this and related duties. They will be assisted by about five hundred metropolitan police from a number of surrounding cities. The parking will be under the direction of about four hundred people employed for this purpose.

Already plans have been made by the railroads to bring 40,000 visitors to Elwood on special trains. One group, which had planned to come six hundred strong has announced that there will be fifteen hundred in the group. Delegations from Missouri, Pennsylvania, New York, Kentucky, Wisconsin, Minnesota, and states further west and south are sponsoring special trains over the railroads. Passengers from the south will be discharged at the Pennsylvania Railroad station; those from the north will be discharged at Ninth Street, where the railroad has constructed long platforms and other station facilities. The special trains from Chicago will have twelve to fourteen cars each and will leave Chicago at frequent intervals, beginning early the morning of August 17.

The Pennsylvania Railroad is expecting to bring in more than forty special cars. The Pullmans will be serviced at Elwood—icing, watering, and air-conditioning; the coaches will be sent to neighboring cities. Four yard engines and a wrecking train will be ready for service here. Fourteen new telegraph stations will be opened between Richmond and Logansport, with thirty-eight extra operators. A public address system will be used at both the permanent and temporary station, and checking facilities will be available at each. All Pennsylvania freight will be routed around on that day. Two doctors, eight uniformed attendants, and fourteen uniformed police will be provided by the railroad company.

The Nickel Plate Railroad is planning twenty special trains for the day. Its Pullmans and coaches will be serviced the same as those on the Pennsylvania Railroad. The regular passenger trains will be run through Elwood as usual, but freight trains will be routed around. Trains for both the railroads will be announced over the public address system at Callaway Park.

The Indiana General Service Company, which provides light and electric power for Elwood, is also making extensive preparations. Current for all concessions will pass through centralized meters. A special transformer and meter will be installed for the Pennsylvania Railroad's lighting and public address system. A ten-horsepower motor will be set up along sidings for the air-conditioning unit on each car held here by the two railroads. Extra transformers are being provided to carry this load.

Motor caravans have also been announced from many points over the nation, especially those not serviced by special trains. One caravan of at least thirty-five large busses will come from Lansing, Michigan. In addition, an immense number of visitors will come in their private cars from a large radius. A section of a new wide highway will be set aside as a temporary airport.

The Pennsylvania Railroad has arranged to bring one group of at least 1500 persons and has arranged to feed this group on a plot south of the park.

Other arrangements for feeding this immense crowd are under way. Of course, the hotels and restaurants of Elwood and surrounding towns will expect to have some share in this; but a large number of concessions stands will be provided. Many homeowners will set up stands on their property. In addition, the Concession and Food Committee will lease concessions both in the downtown districts and within and about the park. No alcoholic liquors will be sold in these concessions. No concessionaires will be permitted to hawk their goods during the program to the annoyance of the listeners.

Everything possible is being done for the convenience of these guests. The speakers' stand will be near the center of the east edge of the park. Tents will be set up on the north and east sides, thirty-six in all, to serve as headquarters for various groups. There will be one for each congressional district, one for the National Republican Committee headquarters, one for the State Republican Committee headquarters, one for the Young Republicans, one for the Colored Voters, one each for the delegations from Ohio, Kentucky, Illinois, and Michigan, four for first aid, two for safety, and tents for the press, sound, and radio workers.

There will be room on the speakers' stand for a thousand persons. West of this platform will be 30,000 chairs. West of this section is a large shaded area through which a great number of benches will be placed. Amplifiers will be so placed that everything said on the platform can be heard as distinctly over a square mile or more as if the listener were beside the speaker. There will also be a radio broadcast.

Incidental to all these activities, but no less important, is the work of the Publicity Committee. It has a direct wire to the Associated Press, International News Service, and United Press Bureaus at Indianapolis. Besides, airmail and special delivery service hurries word of the work all over the country. Reporters visit the headquarters from as far away as the Massachusetts coast. The various other committees keep the Publicity Committee supplied with information about their work, and three people are employed throughout the day and one at night to pass this along.

The communications problem is one of the greatest that the utilities must meet. Until recently, the telegraph office at Elwood has been conducted by one operator and a messenger boy; but the force has already been greatly increased. There has already been an increase of thirty-two in the number of outlets from the local office, and more may be added. The regular office hours have been from eight in the morning until seven at

So That All the World May Know That Elwood Honors Her Son

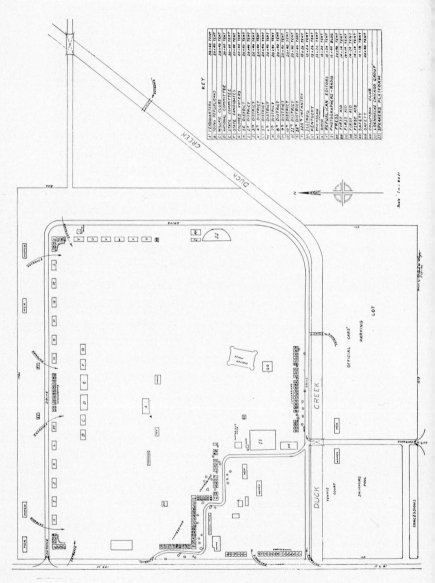

The Site of the Acceptance Speech

night; now they are until eleven at night, and the operators are subject to call at any time. Extra messengers have been put on duty.

On the day of the acceptance speech, the traffic departments from some of the larger cities will send corps of operators capable of sending and receiving by Morse code. Tables will be provided in the office for the press. Radio sets will be established in Callaway park to send messages by radio in the Morse code. These messages will be received by radio and will pass into the regular telegraph system and be received in the regular way.

The telephone company has also made plans to take care of the increased demands. A new ten-mile fifty-one-circuit cable has been built between Elwood and Alexandria. This will connect near Alexandria with outlets at Anderson, Marion, Muncie, and Indianapolis. From Alexandria, additional open-wire circuits have been strung southward for about six miles to connect with the Indianapolis-Anderson-Muncie cable lines.

The radio broadcasting chains will need telephone circuits to carry the speech of acceptance to their transmitters. Telegraph companies, press associations, individual newspapers, and others have requested the Indiana Bell Telephone Company to have private wire facilities ready for their use. At least two representatives of telephoto services will dispatch pictures over the new circuits.

Besides, a large increase in the number of long-distance calls to and from the city is anticipated. Additional public telephones will be installed at convenient locations. It is planned to bring a special portable switchboard, which will be set in a trailer and will have two long-distance operators on duty to assist the regular operators in completing long-distance calls. The telephone company is now prepared to transmit calls to all parts of the world.

The water mains of the town are being extended to the park so that there will be an abundant supply of drinking water. In addition, a large number of thermos tank trucks will be supplied by milk transporters and will be equipped with water fountains.

It is evident that the coming of Wendell Willkie to Elwood is engaging the efforts of a huge force of workers. More than that, it is engaging the interest and hopes of the citizens of his home town, for, after all, he is one of "our boys" to Elwood. From all parts of the country, and even from other lands, will come men and women to do honor to him; but none will do him more loyal or heartfelt honor than those among whom he grew up, who knew his parents, who know his struggles, who have followed his successes, and who now rejoice in this great honor which has come and the still greater honor which they are confident will come to

WENDELL WILLKIE OF ELWOOD.

●

ACKNOWLEDGEMENT

A man with the personality and the ability to make friends which so prominently characterizes Mr. Willkie leaves scattered about in the communities where he visits or makes his home innumerable recollections. These are more revealing than any statistical information about the man or than the published accounts of specific acts that may be found in newspapers or magazines. It is noteworthy that so many of these friends, many from humble walks in life, have been glad to share these recollections with the author so that the bare facts available from public records could be supplemented by the more intimate touches that make a man a human being rather than a collection of statistics. So the hearty co-operation of his many friends, especially in Elwood, his real home, and in Rushville, the early home of his wife, merits this word of appreciation.

So, too, in gathering information about Elwood, the author has been greatly assisted by everyone he has approached. Without question, the citizens of Elwood are proud, and justly so, of the vigor, the intelligence, the civic co-operation, and the common goodwill and good-fellowship of their community.

PRINTED BY DAILY NEWS PUBLISHING CO.
BELOIT, WISCONSIN